BACK TO THE BASICS

FAITH

BACK TO THE BASICS

A Practical Handbook
for Christian Living

Tracy M. Sumner

BARBOUR
PUBLISHING

© 2013 by Barbour Publishing, Inc.

Print ISBN 978-1-62029-760-5

eBook Editions:
Adobe Digital Edition (.epub) 978-1-62416-062-2
Kindle and MobiPocket Edition (.prc) 978-1-62416-061-5

Scripture quotations marked KJV are taken from the King James Version of the Bible.

Scripture quotations marked NKJV are taken from the New King James Version®. Copyright © 1982 by Thomas Nelson, Inc. Used by permission. All rights reserved.

Scripture quotations marked NIV are taken from the HOLY BIBLE, NEW INTERNATIONAL VERSION®. NIV®. Copyright © 1973, 1978, 1984, 2010 by Biblica, Inc.™ Used by permission. All rights reserved worldwide.

Scripture quotations marked NLT are taken from the *Holy Bible.* New Living Translation copyright© 1996, 2004, 2007 by Tyndale House Foundation. Used by permission of Tyndale House Publishers, Inc. Carol Stream, Illinois 60188. All rights reserved.

Scripture quotations marked NASB are taken from the New American Standard Bible, © 1960, 1962, 1963, 1968, 1971, 1972, 1973, 1975, 1977, 1995 by The Lockman Foundation. Used by permission.

Published by Barbour Publishing, Inc., P.O. Box 719, Uhrichsville, Ohio 44683, www.barbourbooks.com

Our mission is to publish and distribute inspirational products offering exceptional value and biblical encouragement to the masses.

 Member of the
Evangelical Christian
Publishers Association

Printed in the United States of America.

CONTENTS

INTRODUCTION

Have you ever stopped and thought—*really* thought—about the word *faith*? In the simplest terms, faith simply means believing in something. It means trusting something or someone to be true and dependable.

Everyone has faith in something—and probably in many things. For example, when we flick on a light switch, we're demonstrating faith that doing so will cause electricity to flow to the light fixtures in a room, allowing us to see what's there. When we engage an automotive ignition switch, we have faith that several of the car's parts will work together and cause its engine to roar to life. And, in a common sermon illustration, when we sit on a chair we have faith that its seat and legs will actually support our weight and keep us from crashing to the floor.

There are endless examples of faith in everyday life. But this little book isn't about that generic brand of faith—it's about faith as it is defined, described, and exemplified in the written Word of God. It's about the kind of faith that allowed the Bible's men and women of God to overcome obstacles—sometimes humanly insurmountable ones—and do great things for their Lord and for other people. And it's about the kind of faith God both gives to and seeks from human beings today.

Christianity is built on a foundation of faith. Christians believe by faith that God exists. They believe by faith that He has performed many miracles. They believe by faith to be saved and receive an eternal home in heaven. By faith, they are made more like Jesus Christ, and by faith they accomplish great things for God's kingdom.

Scripture records dozens and dozens of promises, and God has designed that we appropriate those promises through faith. To put that another way, we can only claim and live in God's wonderful promises when we have faith in Him—in His absolute trustworthiness, goodness, and dependability in keeping those promises.

This book is about that kind of faith.

As you read, you'll learn what true biblical faith really is—and what that kind of faith can do for you and your relationship with God. You'll see amazing examples of world-changing faith—including that of the perfect Man of Faith, Jesus Christ—and learn how you can develop a stronger, deeper faith.

Faith: Back to the Basics directly quotes many, many scripture verses and passages. That is no accident. The apostle Paul wrote that "faith comes by hearing, and hearing by the word of God" (Romans 10:17 NKJV). This verse teaches, in essence, that we acquire faith by hearing (or reading) and understanding the written Word of God.

In a book of this size, it isn't possible to print everything the Bible has to say about faith. Our hope is that you'll use this book as a jumping-off point to a deeper, wider examination of what God wants to teach you about *faith*.

1

WHY FAITH?

Faith is the root of all blessings. Believe, and you shall be saved; believe, and you must needs be satisfied; believe, and you cannot but be comforted and happy.
JEREMY TAYLOR

How would you respond if a friend said something like this to you: "I believe that if I live a good life, treat other people right, and try to help others who aren't as fortunate, then I'll go to heaven someday. I believe God keeps a balance sheet on everyone, and if we do more good than bad in this life, we'll be okay."

No one would rightly discourage another human from living a moral life or doing good things for other people. But the Bible-believing Christian knows that those things alone—important as they are—cannot make a man or woman right with God. They can't guarantee a person a place in heaven.

True, the Bible is filled with instructions for living a good life. But it's also filled with God's call for people to relate to Him on the basis of faith. The writer of Hebrews states it very clearly: "But without faith it is impossible to please Him, for he who comes to God must believe that He is, and that He is a rewarder of those who diligently seek Him" (Hebrews 11:6 NKJV).

Reread that verse and focus on the word *impossible*. In a chapter that repeatedly shows that with faith we can do what no one can accomplish through human strength alone, that one word stands out.

Impossible, as in something that absolutely, positively cannot be done.

Without faith, there is nothing we can do to make ourselves "good enough" to please our Creator. Without faith, the very best we have to offer God will never be acceptable to Him. We could stand out in the world as humanitarians doing great things for other people, pouring our lives into making a better world—but without faith, it wouldn't be enough.

The prophet Isaiah underscored this fact when he wrote, "All of us have become like one who is unclean, and all our righteous acts are like filthy rags; we all shrivel up like a leaf, and like the wind our sins sweep us away" (Isaiah 64:6 NIV).

We can be grateful the story doesn't stop there. When we come to God believing that He really is, when we make our life's goal to seek Him and know Him for what He really is, then we receive His incredible rewards—both here on earth and in the life to come.

Created for Faith

If you read through the Bible, you'll begin to understand the kind of relationship God seeks with His creation. You'll see very plainly that God desires (even seeks out) a relationship with individual humans based on faith—our faith in Him. You might even say we were created for faith.

This truth was demonstrated as far back as the Garden of Eden. The first three chapters of Genesis give the account of God's creation of our world (and the whole universe), of His relationship with the first two humans (His most prized creation), and of those humans' fall into sin that broke their connection with God.

At first, the relationship between God and the first two people—Adam and his wife, Eve— was an absolutely perfect picture of faith. God provided everything the people needed to live. Adam and Eve enjoyed a wonderful fellowship with each other and with God. God gave these two humans free run of the Garden of Eden. They could do what they wanted and eat what they wanted—with just one exception:

> *The LORD God took the man and put him in the Garden of Eden to work it and take care of it. And the LORD God commanded the man, "You are free to eat from any tree in the garden; but*

you must not eat from the tree of the knowledge of good and evil, for when you eat from it you will certainly die."

GENESIS 2:15–17 NIV

Things changed dramatically for Adam and Eve—and all future humanity—after the serpent tempted them. This serpent, actually the devil in snake's clothing, called into question the two humans' faith in God.

The first question was whether or not Eve and her husband could truly trust God: "Did God really say, 'You must not eat from any tree in the garden'?" the serpent asked (Genesis 3:1 NIV). Eve knew very well that God had said she and Adam were not to eat from the "tree of the knowledge of good and evil" (Genesis 2:17)—but the serpent put a clever spin on what God had said, thus calling into question God's trustworthiness. The devil wanted Eve to believe that God was holding out on her and Adam. By commanding them not to eat from that one tree, the devil implied, God didn't have Adam and Eve's best interest at heart.

Tragically, the humans gave in to the devil's temptation, ending their perfect faith-and-fellowship relationship with their Creator. With that one decision, the world's first humans chose their own way over a perfect life of reliance on and obedience to their Creator.

Since that moment—which theologians and Bible scholars call "the Fall"—sin has broken the relationship between God and humankind. The apostle Paul wrote of this "original sin," as it has been called: "Therefore, just as sin entered the world through one man, and death through sin. . .in this way death came to all people, because all sinned" (Romans 5:12 NIV).

Since the Fall, only one thing differentiates those who belong to God and those who don't: faith. In the context of Genesis 2–3, those with true faith in God see life from a "God has said" perspective. Those who lack faith view life from a "Did God really say?" point of view.

Faith is what saves us and guarantees us a place in God's eternal kingdom. Faith is what sets us apart from the rest of the world, allowing us to live a life that pleases God. And it's the basis for every blessing from God—both in this life and in eternity.

God longs to bless those who walk in faith, the people who so fully trust Him that their lives become brilliant reflections of His character, ways, and desires.

The Eternal Rewards of Faith

When you read words such as *faith* or *believe* in the Bible, they usually refer to one of two things: the faith or belief leading to eternal salvation and the faith or belief needed to live a life that pleases God—and to accomplish great things for God.

Let's take a quick look at the eternal ramifications of true biblical faith.

The Bible lists several things God does for us when we simply believe Him and receive His promise of salvation through faith in Jesus Christ. Through this kind of faith, we are:

- Justified (made right with God)—
"Through him everyone who believes is
set free from every sin, a justification you
were not able to obtain under the law of
Moses" (Acts 13:39 NIV; also see Romans
3:21–22, 28, 30; Galatians 2:16).

- Saved from eternal
condemnation—"Whoever believes
and is baptized will be saved, but whoever
does not believe will be condemned"
(Mark 16:16 NIV; also see Acts 16:31).

- Brought into spiritual light—"Believe
in the light while you have the light, so
that you may become children of light. . . .
I have come into the world as a light, so
that no one who believes in me should
stay in darkness" (John 12:36, 46 NIV).

- Given spiritual life—"But these are
written, that ye might believe that Jesus
is the Christ, the Son of God; and that
believing ye might have life through
his name" (John 20:31 KJV; also see
Galatians 2:20).

- Given eternal life—"Whoever believes in Him should not perish but have eternal life. For God so loved the world that He gave His only begotten Son, that whoever believes in Him should not perish but have everlasting life" (John 3:15–16 NKJV; also see John 6:40, 47).

- Given eternal rest—"Now we who have believed enter that rest, just as God has said, 'So I declared on oath in my anger, "They shall never enter my rest."' And yet his works have been finished since the creation of the world" (Hebrews 4:3 NIV).

- Preserved for eternal salvation—". . .who are protected by the power of God through faith for a salvation ready to be revealed in the last time" (1 Peter 1:5 NASB).

- Adopted into God's family—"But as many as received Him, to them He gave the right to become children of God, even to those who believe in His name" (John 1:12 NASB; also see Galatians 3:26).

- Given access to God—"In him and through faith in him we may approach God with freedom and confidence" (Ephesians 3:12 NIV).

- Made recipients of everything God has promised—"But the Scripture has confined all under sin, that the promise by faith in Jesus Christ might be given to those who believe" (Galatians 3:22 NKJV).

- Given God's Holy Spirit—"And as I began to speak, the Holy Spirit fell upon them just as He did upon us at the beginning. And I remembered the word of the Lord, how He used to say, 'John baptized with water, but you will be baptized with the Holy Spirit.' Therefore if God gave to them the same gift as He gave to us also after believing in the Lord Jesus Christ, who was I that I could stand in God's way?" (Acts 11:15–17 NASB; also see Galatians 3:14; Ephesians 1:13).

For those whose faith is in Jesus Christ, these are all amazing promises for their eternal salvation. But faith isn't just a way to spend forever in a heavenly paradise with God. The Bible also contains many promises for the life of faith here on earth.

Faith: A Way of Life for Believers

While there are many ancient examples of people whose faith in God moved them to obey Him and do amazing things for Him, the word *faith* itself appears just a few times in the Old Testament. In the King James Bible, the term appears in the Old Testament just twice. There are four uses of *faith* in the New American Standard Version and fewer than twenty in the New International Version and the New Revised Standard Version.

Does that mean that faith somehow became more important during New Testament times? Did God require people in the Old Testament era to earn their salvation through the good things they did? Did God decide to make faith the basis of eternal life later on? Absolutely not!

The fact is, the theme of faith runs throughout the Old Testament (you'll read more about that in Chapter 6)—even if the word itself is hard to find in the first thirty-three books of the Bible.

One of the few Old Testament instances of the word *faith* is found in the writings of a relatively obscure prophet named Habakkuk. He wrote, "Behold the proud, his soul is not upright in him; but the just shall live by his faith" (Habakkuk 2:4 NKJV).

That single Old Testament reference is one of the most important statements the entire Bible makes on the subject of faith in the life of a believer. It lays out a strong contrast between the proud and self-sufficient (including those who believe that being "good" will make them right with God) and those whose who live their lives—*every part* of their lives—by faith in the living God. Habakkuk made such an impression on New Testament writers that he is directly quoted in three different passages: Romans 1:17,

Galatians 3:11, and Hebrews 10:38.

The apostle Paul shared essentially the same message when he wrote, "we walk by faith, not by sight" (2 Corinthians 5:7 KJV). In this context, the word *walk* means to live by faith, to put faith in God at the very center of every part of your life as a believer: spiritual life, work life, family life, social life. . .the list goes on and on.

Jesus taught His disciples the vital importance of continuing to live in faith after salvation: "I am the vine; you are the branches. If you remain in me and I in you, you will bear much fruit; apart from me you can do nothing" (John 15:5 NIV).

If you embrace the teachings of Jesus Christ concerning faith—and as you'll see later in this book, you certainly should!—you can take His words to heart and understand that there is no way you can do anything positive for God or anyone else unless you live by faith.

Without faith it is impossible to please God. Without faith it is impossible to gain eternal life in heaven. Without faith it is impossible to mature and grow as a Christian. And without faith it is impossible to accomplish anything of value for God's kingdom.

With faith, however, you can do all the things listed above and more. As Jesus promised His followers those many centuries ago, "all things are possible with God" (Mark 10:27 NIV).

The Bible says much more about believers living and walking in faith. When we live by faith, scripture teaches, we will be able to:

- Live life in our physical bodies—"I have been crucified with Christ and I no longer live, but Christ lives in me. The life I now live in the body, I live by faith in the Son of God, who loved me and gave himself for me" (Galatians 2:20 NIV).

- Stand firm—"Not that we lord it over your faith, but we work with you for your joy, because it is by faith you stand firm" (2 Corinthians 1:24 NIV).

- Accomplish the humanly impossible—"So Jesus said to them, 'Because of your unbelief; for assuredly, I say to you, if you have faith as a mustard seed, you will say to this mountain, "Move from here to there," and it will move; and nothing will be impossible for you'" (Matthew 17:20 NKJV).

- Receive wisdom—"But if any of you lacks wisdom, let him ask of God, who gives to all generously and without reproach, and it will be given to him. But he must ask in faith without any doubting, for the one who doubts is like the surf of the sea, driven and tossed by the wind. For that man ought not to expect that he will receive anything from the Lord, being a double-minded man, unstable in all his ways" (James 1:5–8 NASB).

- Be edified (built up and strengthened)—"Nor give heed to fables and endless genealogies, which cause disputes rather than godly edification which is in faith" (1 Timothy 1:4 NKJV; also see Jude 20)

- Overcome the world—"For whatever is born of God overcomes the world; and this is the victory that has overcome the world—our faith. Who is the one who overcomes the world, but he who believes that Jesus is the Son of God?" (1 John 5:4–5 NASB).

- Resist the devil—"Be alert and of sober mind. Your enemy the devil prowls around like a roaring lion looking for someone to devour. Resist him, standing firm in the faith, because you know that the family of believers throughout the world is undergoing the same kind of sufferings" (1 Peter 5:8–9 NIV).

- Receive answers to prayer—"And whatever things you ask in prayer, believing, you will receive" (Matthew 21:22 NKJV).

- Defend ourselves against the devil—"In addition to all this, take up the shield of faith, with which you can extinguish all the flaming arrows of the evil one" (Ephesians 6:16 NIV).

- Receive encouragement—"I would have lost heart, unless I had believed that I would see the goodness of the LORD in the land of the living" (Psalm 27:13 NKJV).

There is no question that faith is the very center of the Christian life. Faith is what saves us, what helps us grow as believers, and what allows us to do what otherwise couldn't be done through human strength alone.

2

DEFINING TRUE BIBLICAL FAITH

"Let God be true but every man a liar"
is the language of true faith.
A.W. Tozer

You just read in Chapter 1 why God wants you to have faith in Him, why it's important for the believer have faith, and what faith does in and for you. Now let's define what true biblical faith really is.

First of all, faith is at the very heart of Christianity. It's safe to say that there is no more important aspect of the Christian life than faith. The Bible teaches that it is faith that leads and enables us to live the way God wants us to live. And we cannot even have a relationship with God without faith.

But what exactly is it? Before we explain what true biblical faith is, let's look at what it is *not*. The simple truth of the matter is that too many people—including some Bible-believing Christians—have fallen into confusion about true faith.

Biblical Faith—What It Isn't

Whenever God creates something beautiful and perfect—as He did when He designed true faith in Him—you can be sure that the devil will do everything he can to divert attention from it, misrepresent it, or create a counterfeit for it. The enemy of our souls has most certainly been busy attacking faith.

There are many counterfeits to true biblical faith, and it's important that we understand *why* they are frauds.

Biblical faith is not:

1. *Simply believing in God.* Faith as it is defined in the Bible isn't merely believing that

there is a God. That's certainly a part of faith, and a great place to start. But most people believe there is a god of some sort, a creator of all they see around them. That does show a level of faith, but not biblical faith.

The apostle James warned that believing in the God of the Bible isn't the equivalent of true saving faith: "You believe that there is one God. You do well. Even the demons believe—and tremble!" (James 2:19 NKJV).

The writer of Hebrews stated that people who want to please God must believe that He exists—but he also wrote that they must also believe that "he rewards those who earnestly seek him" (Hebrews 11:6 NIV).

So true biblical faith includes earnestly and persistently seeking God—the one true God, as He has identified Himself in the Bible—knowing that He will reward that persistence.

2. *Adhering to a system of beliefs or doctrines.* True biblical faith isn't just mental agreement with the tenets of Christianity. That is not to say that doctrine (which we can roughly define as the principles, guidelines, and commands

laid out in the Bible) isn't important. Of course it is.

The apostle Paul underscored the importance of sound doctrine when he encouraged a young pastor named Timothy to "Watch your life and doctrine closely. Persevere in them, because if you do, you will save both yourself and your hearers" (1 Timothy 4:16 NIV).

Paul also wrote to a young man named Titus, pastor of the church at Crete, that a Christian leader must "hold firmly to the trustworthy message as it has been taught, so that he can encourage others by sound doctrine and refute those who oppose it" (Titus 1:9 NIV). He also wrote to Titus, "You, however, must teach what is appropriate to sound doctrine" (Titus 2:1 NIV).

Good doctrine is vitally important because it defines what we as Christians believe. But a person can quote absolutely sound Christian doctrine and still lack the kind of faith that guarantees them a place in God's eternal kingdom.

3. *Taking part in religious observances and*

practices. Many Christian churches engage in various observances, some of which have their roots in many centuries of tradition. But it's important to understand that these things, in and of themselves, do not constitute true faith.

Jesus repeatedly chided the religious leaders of His day for holding to doctrines and rules—and forcing others to do the same—while missing true faith in and love for God. In other words, these people cared more about their own religion than they did about God—or other people. That's not what God calls real faith!

Years later, the apostle Paul warned believers in Colossae, "Beware lest any man spoil you through philosophy and vain deceit, after the tradition of men, after the rudiments of the world, and not after Christ" (Colossians 2:8 KJV).

Does this mean that all Christian observances and traditions are wrong? Not at all. Some are firmly based on the written Word of God, and we observe them out of obedience—for example, baptism and the

Lord's Supper. But we can never allow rituals to take the place of true personal faith.

4. *Feelings or "blind faith."* The apostle Paul wrote that "we live by faith, not by sight" (2 Corinthians 5:7 NIV). Real biblical faith is not based on what we see—1 John 4:12 points out that no one has ever seen God. Nor does true biblical faith grow out of our feelings. True faith rests on evidence presented in the Bible.

Feelings can be deceptive, and "blind faith" (believing in something though there is no evidence that's true) isn't helpful, either. That is why the Bible encourages believers to read and study scripture to know what it teaches.

The apostle John recorded the great works of Jesus in the fourth Gospel so that "you may continue to believe that Jesus is the Messiah, the Son of God, and that by believing in him you will have life by the power of his name" (John 20:31 NLT). When the apostle Paul wrote "faith cometh by hearing, and hearing by the word of God" (Romans 10:17 KJV), he was pointing out that real faith is based on the truth of scripture.

5. *Simply being sincere in what you believe.* We've all heard it said: "It really doesn't matter what you place your faith in, as long as you're sincere in what you believe." As far as God is concerned, this thinking goes, *sincerity* is the key to a relationship with Him and eternal salvation.

Everyone has faith in something. Even atheists exercise a certain level of faith—the faith that there is no God. Hindus, Buddhists, Muslims, and adherents to many other religions also exercise faith, sometimes a very strong one. Some people put their faith in their own good living, believing that being a good person is enough in God's eyes.

But when it comes to where a person will spend eternity, the question is not the sincerity of one's faith, but in what or whom the faith is placed in. Christians are people who have placed their faith in the finished work of Jesus Christ on the cross.

How would you define the word *faith*? Most Christians understand that their relationship with God is based on faith—but many would have a difficult time defining the word.

We've already discussed what faith is not—but what *is* it? You can find these definitions on the web site Oxforddictionaries.com: "Complete trust or confidence in someone or something" and "strong belief in the doctrines of a religion, based on spiritual conviction rather than proof."

The Bible contains this simple definition of faith: "Now faith is confidence in what we hope for and assurance about what we do not see" (Hebrews 11:1 NIV).

Three key words in this verse—*confidence, hope,* and *assurance*—will help us to fully understand what the Bible means by the word *faith*:

1. *Confidence*: In modern times, people use the word *confidence* almost as a substitute for phrases such as "I'm pretty sure" or "This is how I believe it will go." People often voice

confidence over things such as the results of an election or the outcome of this weekend's big game. But guess what? Things don't always go the way we think they will—sometimes the other candidate wins or the football underdog pulls off an upset. Confidence in God's promises, though, will never disappoint us. In Hebrews 11:1, that confidence is absolute. In fact, some Bible translations use words denoting *absolute* confidence or conviction that what God has promised, He will also fulfill.

2. *Hope*: We've all heard people talk about things they wish to happen using the word *hope*, as in "I hope I can find a new job" or "I hope my son recovers from his illness soon." However, the word as it is used in Hebrews 11:1 means something far more wonderful for the believer. As Christians, the objects of our hope are the promises God has made in His written Word, the Bible. When we say we have put our hope in God's promises, we're not saying we *wish* for them to be fulfilled; rather, we're saying we look forward to the

time when they become reality.

3. *Assurance*: The writer of the book of Hebrews uses this word in relation to the things we believe but have not seen. For example, no one has seen God, no one was around to witness the creation of the world, and very few saw the newly resurrected Jesus Christ (certainly no one alive today has). Yet, through faith we believe in each, simply because they are recorded in the pages of scripture. Our assurance also applies to those things God has promised but which have not yet happened. You can know with assurance, for example, that God will meet all your spiritual and physical needs (Philippians 4:19), that He has your future mapped out (Jeremiah 29:11), and that you will spend eternity in heaven (Romans 6:23).

Faith. . .in the Right Things

Earlier in this chapter, you read how *sincerity of belief* is not the same as true biblical faith. As someone has pointed out, you can be sincere in your beliefs, but sincerely wrong.

Sincerity in what we believe isn't a bad thing—in fact, it's essential to a growing, thriving faith. But for faith to be true and biblical, it must be aligned with the standards laid out in scripture.

So what are we as Christians to place our faith in? The Bible actually lists several persons/things we are to hold to in faith:

- God—"Don't let your hearts be troubled. Trust in God, and trust also in me" (John 14:1 NLT)

- Jesus Christ—"Jesus answered and said unto them, This is the work of God, that ye believe on him whom he hath sent" (John 6:29 KJV; also see Acts 20:21).

- Writings of Moses—"For had ye believed Moses, ye would have believed me; for he wrote of me" (John 5:46 KJV; also see Acts 24:14).

- Writings of the prophets—"Early in the morning they left for the Desert of Tekoa. As they set out, Jehoshaphat stood and said, 'Listen to me, Judah and people of Jerusalem! Have faith in the LORD your God and you will be upheld; have faith in his prophets and you will be successful'" (2 Chronicles 20:20 NIV; also see Acts 26:27)

- The Gospel—"The time has come," he said. "The kingdom of God has come near. Repent and believe the good news!" (Mark 1:15 NIV).

- The promises of God—". . .being fully persuaded that God had power to do what he had promised" (Romans 4:21 NIV; also see Hebrews 11:13).

You can absolutely count on God to save you and give you what you need to live a life of growing, overcoming faith—when you place your faith in the right things. God keeps His promises—all His promises—as recorded in the pages of the Bible.

What Is "Saving Faith?"

The Bible describes two kinds of faith: the kind needed for salvation and the kind believers need to accomplish anything for God. Saving faith is described very simply in the book of Acts: "Believe in the Lord Jesus, and you will be saved" (16:31 NIV).

Saving faith is described very simply in the Bible. It is not a complicated process with a list of tasks God requires—but neither is it merely simply believing that a man named Jesus existed and that He died for our sins. That is a mere "head knowledge"—and while it's important, it's not what God means when He said to "believe in the Lord Jesus Christ."

In its original language as it appears in the New Testament, the word *believe* as it relates to saving faith means much more than just mental agreement. It carries with it the idea of commitment, trust, and reliance. It means agreeing with God's Word that sin eternally separates us from God, that we are sinners, and that He has provided one way—and one way only—for us to receive salvation and eternal life. It means personalizing all these truths—as in, *I* am a sinner and can do nothing to receive God's forgiveness and that Jesus Christ died for *me* so that *I* can be saved.

If someone were to ask how you know you are saved, what would you say? If you are truly saved, you will not point to anything you have done or not done. On the contrary, you will answer without hesitation: "I am saved only because of what Jesus Christ did for me."

True saving faith must have as its object the Lord Jesus Christ. Jesus Himself said, "I am the way and the truth and the life. No one comes to the Father except through me" (John 14:6 NIV). The apostle Peter, speaking before the Jewish religious council in Jerusalem not long after Jesus returned to heaven, echoed that exclusive message when he said, "Salvation is found in no one else, for there is no other name under heaven given to mankind by which we must be saved" (Acts 4:12 NIV).

Childlike Faith

Someone has said that there is no better illustration of faith than a small child. Many parents have learned (sometimes the hard way) that a child will believe anything you tell him—and that he will often repeat what he has been told.

A child who lives in a healthy environment has faith that his parents will love him, provide for him, and care for him. He doesn't question those things or wonder how or when they are coming—he just knows they are. He believes his parents when they make him a promise; he knows they will do as they have said.

One day, when people began bringing their children to Jesus for His blessing on them, the Lord tapped into the beauty of childlike faith. The disciples wanted to keep the children away, but Jesus scolded the men, telling them to allow the children to come. Then Jesus used the occasion to teach them and others nearby an important lesson about faith.

"Let the little children come to me, and

do not hinder them," Jesus said, "for the kingdom of God belongs to such as these. Truly I tell you, anyone who will not receive the kingdom of God like a little child will never enter it" (Luke 18:16–17 NIV).

Jesus' statement—that those who refuse to receive the eternal kingdom of God like small children will never enter it—should certainly catch our attention. He was teaching that our faith in Him is not just a mental assent to the truths He taught or to the promises that fill the pages of scripture. Of course it's important to know Jesus' teachings and God's promises, but the key is whether or not we truly and personally *trust* them.

A young believer was once asked why he was absolutely confident that he would spend eternity in heaven. His answer wasn't made up of deep, complicated theology, and it didn't include any mention of what he had done or not done as qualification. It was simply this: "I believe that God always keeps His promises."

That is what childlike faith looks like. It is a simple confidence that, no matter what else may happen, God can be trusted to keep each and every promise He has made. It is approaching Him with an outstretched, empty hand—knowing that we, like small children, have nothing to offer Him but the confidence that He will grant us everything He has promised to give us if we only believe Him.

The apostle Paul touched on the idea of childlike faith when he wrote, "For you did not receive the spirit of bondage again to fear, but you received the Spirit of adoption by whom we cry out, 'Abba, Father'" (Romans 8:15 NKJV). In its original language, the word *Abba* in this verse denotes a deeply personal, loving relationship—much like that of a loving earthly father to his children. It is roughly the equivalent of the modern English word *daddy*.

True faith, as defined in the Bible, is a simple heart attitude of trust—the kind of trust a small child has in its parents. It is a mind-set that says, "On my own, I can't do anything—I can't be saved, can't know God, can't become a better person, can't accomplish anything of lasting or eternal significance. But my Father in heaven can—and because I trust Him to keep His promises, He'll do all those things for me."

3

JESUS: THE ULTIMATE EXAMPLE OF FAITH

"By myself I can do nothing; I judge only as I hear, and my judgment is just, for I seek not to please myself but him who sent me."
JESUS CHRIST (JOHN 5:30 NIV)

The book of Hebrews defines faith as "the substance of things hoped for, the evidence of things not seen" (Hebrews 11:1 NKJV). As amazing as that one-sentence definition of true biblical faith is, it is not the only one found within scripture.

If you want to see the perfect example—the perfect *definition*—of faith in the Bible, you need look no further than the four Gospels, which record the words and actions of the Lord Jesus Christ.

Many excellent examples of faith can be found in both the Old and New Testaments. But all of these examples feature imperfect human beings who went through moments when their faith faltered—when it wasn't everything it should have been.

Not so with Jesus. He was the ultimate man of faith. Everything Jesus did and said during His earthly ministry was bathed in an unshakable faith in His heavenly Father. He acted in faith, spoke in faith, taught about faith, responded to the faith of people He encountered, and lovingly but sternly rebuked His closest friends for their weakness of faith. Jesus lived a life of total dependence on His Father in heaven. When He spoke, He spoke the words of God (John 14:10). When He performed a miracle, He did it though the power from above (Acts 2:22). When He went to the cross to pay for the sins of all humankind, He did so in faith (Luke 22:41–42).

Speaking to a group of very critical Jewish religious leaders, Jesus said, "Very truly I tell you, the Son can do nothing by himself; he can do only what he sees his Father doing, because whatever the Father does the Son also does. For the Father loves the Son and shows him all he does. Yes, and he will show him even greater works than these, so that you will be amazed" (John 5:19–20 NIV).

That statement alone was an amazing demonstration of Jesus' faith in His heavenly Father. First of all, it clearly demonstrated the fact that Jesus knew who He was (the Son of God) and that He was completely dependent upon His Father. Second, it demonstrated His faith inspired courage, for He knew that speaking of Himself as God's Son was sure to get Him in trouble with these religious leaders.

The Bible states that "without faith it is impossible to please God" (Hebrews 11:6 NIV). Everything Jesus did and said pleased God, which the Father Himself declared at Jesus' baptism: "This is My beloved Son, in whom I am *well pleased*" (Matthew 3:17 NKJV, emphasis added).

The Bible's big-picture definition of faith is total and unwavering trust in God in every area of our lives. Jesus perfectly exemplified that kind of faith—in fact, He was the only man ever to live out perfect faith in the heavenly Father. God was pleased that Jesus exhibited that kind of faith, and He is pleased with us when we follow Jesus' example. That is what the apostle Paul meant when he wrote, "you should imitate me, just as I imitate Christ" (1 Corinthians 11:1 NLT).

If you've ever read through the four Gospels (if you haven't, make the time to do so as soon as possible!), you may have noticed that Jesus never hesitated to obey God, never wondered whether or not God had given Him the power and authority to do the things He did, never voiced even the slightest bit of doubt. When He had an opportunity to do or say something to glorify His Father in heaven, He simply did it.

Jesus could do and say the things He did because He possessed a perfect faith in God. He was the perfect picture of faith and a perfect picture of the kind of obedience to God that real faith always produces.

"I Am". . .the Perfect Man of Faith

One thing faith does in the life of believers is give them identity—a sense of who they are in Christ. Because Jesus was the perfect man of faith, He had a perfect sense of His own identity. That sense of identity allowed Him to confidently let others know just who He was and why He had come to earth.

He shared His identity through several "I am" statements:

- "I am the bread of life. Whoever comes to me will never go hungry, and whoever believes in me will never be thirsty" (John 6:35 NIV).

- "I am the living bread that came down from heaven. Whoever eats this bread will live forever" (John 6:51 NIV).

- "I am the light of the world. If you follow me, you won't have to walk in darkness, because you will have the light that leads to life" (John 8:12 NLT)

- "You are from below; I am from above. You belong to this world; I do not. That is why I said that you will die in your sins; for unless you believe that I Am who I claim to be, you will die in your sins" (John 8:23–24 NLT).

- "Most assuredly, I say to you, before Abraham was, I AM" (John 8:58 NKJV).

- "Truly, truly, I say to you, I am the door of the sheep. All who came before Me are thieves and robbers, but the sheep did not hear them. I am the door; if anyone enters through Me, he will be saved, and will go in and out and find pasture" (John 10:7–9 NASB).

- "I am the good shepherd; the good shepherd lays down His life for the sheep" (John 10:11 NASB).

- "Do you say of Him, whom the Father sanctified and sent into the world, 'You are blaspheming,' because I said, 'I am the Son of God'?" (John 10:36 NASB).

- "I am the resurrection and the life. The one who believes in me will live, even though they die; and whoever lives by believing in me will never die" (John 11:25–26 NIV).

- "I am the way and the truth and the life. No one comes to the Father except through me" (John 14:6 NIV).

- "I am the true vine, and my Father is the gardener. . . . I am the vine; you are the branches. If you remain in me and I in you, you will bear much fruit; apart from me you can do nothing" (John 15:1, 5 NIV).

Jesus' statements of His personal identity might come across as audacious—maybe even presumptuous—but for this important truth: Jesus knew exactly who He was because He had perfect faith in His Father in heaven. He could courageously answer His many critics with this amazing declaration of His true identity: "Even if I bear witness of Myself, My witness is true, for I know where I came from and where I am going; but you do not know where I come from and where I am going. You judge according to the flesh; I judge no one. And yet if I do judge, My judgment is true; for I am not alone, but I am with the Father who sent Me" (John 8:14–16 NKJV).

It was the same kind of faith that allowed Jesus to pray, with absolute confidence, "Father, I thank you that you have heard me. I knew that you always hear me, but I said this for the benefit of the people standing here, that they may believe that you sent me" (John 11:41–42 NIV).

Jesus' Own Words about Faith

Jesus had much to say on the subject of faith. As the "author and finisher of our faith" (Hebrews 12:2 NKJV), and as a man who perfectly "walked the walk," He was able to speak on the subject with amazing authority. Sometimes He instructed and encouraged His followers to live lives of faith, sometimes He encouraged them to grow in their faith, and sometimes He firmly scolded others (including those who were very close to Him) for their lack of faith.

Here are some of the things He said on this vital subject:

- "You of little faith. . .why did you doubt?" (Matthew 14:31 NIV).

- "O faithless and perverse generation, how long shall I be with you? How long shall I bear with you?" (Matthew 17:17 NKJV).

- "Assuredly, I say to you, if you have faith as a mustard seed, you will say to this mountain, 'Move from here to there,' and it will move; and nothing will be impossible for you" (Matthew 17:20 NKJV).

- "And all things you ask in prayer, believing, you will receive" (Matthew 21:22 NASB).

- "Why are you afraid? Do you still have no faith?" (Mark 4:40 NLT).

- "Do not be afraid; only believe" (Mark 5:36 NKJV).

- "Everything is possible for one who believes" (Mark 9:23 NIV).

- "Have faith in God. For assuredly, I say to you, whoever says to this mountain, 'Be removed and be cast into the sea,' and does not doubt in his heart, but believes that those things he says will be done, he will have whatever he says. Therefore I say to you, whatever things you ask when you pray, believe that you receive them, and you will have them" (Mark 11:22–24 NKJV).

- "These signs will accompany those who have believed: in My name they will cast out demons, they will speak with new tongues; they will pick up serpents, and if they drink any deadly poison, it will not hurt them; they will lay hands on the sick, and they will recover" (Mark 16:17–18 NASB).

- "If you have faith as a mustard seed, you can say to this mulberry tree, 'Be pulled up by the roots and be planted in the sea,' and it would obey you" (Luke 17:6 NKJV).

- "When the Son of Man comes, will he find faith on the earth?" (Luke 18:8 NIV).

- "O foolish men and slow of heart to believe in all that the prophets have spoken! Was it not necessary for the Christ to suffer these things and to enter into His glory?" (Luke 24:25–26 NASB).

- "Why are you troubled? And why do doubts arise in your hearts?" (Luke 24:38 NKJV).

- "For God so loved the world that he gave his one and only Son, that whoever believes in him shall not perish but have eternal life" (John 3:16 NIV).

- "He who believes in Him is not judged; he who does not believe has been judged already, because he has not believed in the name of the only begotten Son of God" (John 3:18 NASB).

- "He who believes in the Son has eternal life; but he who does not obey the Son will not see life, but the wrath of God abides on him" (John 3:36 NASB).

- "Truly, truly, I say to you, he who believes has eternal life" (John 6:47 NASB).

- "He who believes in Me, believes not in Me but in Him who sent Me" (John 12:44 NKJV).

- "Do not let your heart be troubled; believe in God, believe also in Me. In My Father's house are many dwelling places; if it were not so, I would have told you; for I go to prepare a place for you" (John 14:1–2 NASB).

- "Believe Me that I am in the Father and the Father is in Me" (John 14:11 NASB).

- "Very truly I tell you, whoever believes in me will do the works I have been doing, and they will do even greater things than these, because I am going to the Father" (John 14:12 NIV).

- "Whoever believes and is baptized will be saved, but whoever does not believe will be condemned" (Mark 16:16 NIV).

- "I am praying not only for these disciples but also for all who will ever believe in me through their message. I pray that they will all be one, just as you and I are one—as you are in me, Father, and I am in you. And may they be in us so that the world will believe you sent me" (John 17:20–21 NLT).

- "Because you have seen me, you have believed; blessed are those who have not seen and yet have believed" (John 20:29 NIV).

There never has been—nor will there ever be—a human being who walked, talked, and taught the life of faith like Jesus did. And while we as imperfect human beings will never match Jesus' level of faith, we can follow His perfect example and learn from His teachings.

4

SALVATION: IT ALL STARTS WITH FAITH

Genuine faith that saves the soul has for its main element—trust—absolute rest of the whole soul—on the Lord Jesus Christ to save me, whether He died in particular or in special to save me or not, and relying, as I am, wholly and alone on Him, I am saved.

CHARLES SPURGEON

The book of Acts is an amazing collection of stories about the establishment of the Christian church following Jesus' return to heaven. It gives the accounts of the powerful faith of many men (and a few specific women) and what that faith allowed them to accomplish for the kingdom of God.

One of those stories describes the apostle Paul and his traveling companion, Silas, being miraculously delivered from a prison cell in Philippi (Acts 16:16–34). Though the two men had been badly beaten, thrown in jail, and restrained with stocks on their feet, they stayed strong in their faith. Rather than complaining about their predicament, they loudly sang praises to God—and the other prisoners and their jailer listened in.

Then, around midnight, a miracle happened: An earthquake struck, shaking the very foundation of the prison and popping open its doors. When the guard awoke, he saw all the doors ajar and assumed Paul and Silas had fled into the night. Knowing the trouble he faced for allowing prisoners to escape, the jailer drew his sword to end his own life.

But Paul and Silas hadn't gone anywhere. Sensing that the guard was about to commit suicide, Paul called out from the cell, urging him not to harm himself because the prisoners were still in the jail.

It's hard to say what made a bigger

impression on this guard: The fact that Paul and Silas prayed and sang to God after being beaten and jailed, or that they stayed in their cell when they could just as easily have made a quick getaway from the jail *and* the city.

Either way, jailer saw something in Paul and Silas that he wanted for himself. He had personally witnessed them putting action behind their faith—he knew they were the genuine article. "Sirs, what must I do to be saved?" he asked (Acts 16:30 NKJV).

It was the simple but all-important question each of us must ask ourselves at some point in life. And Paul and Silas had an equally simple and all-important answer: "Believe on the Lord Jesus Christ, and you will be saved, you and your household" (Acts 16:31 NKJV).

The New Testament is filled with references to the wonderful message of salvation through faith—through truly believing in and relying on the Lord Jesus Christ. But this promise of salvation through faith didn't suddenly appear with the arrival of Jesus Christ or the start of the New Testament Church. On the contrary, its first biblical mention appears early in the book of Genesis: "Abram believed the LORD, and he credited it to him as righteousness" (Genesis 15:6 NIV).

Following are several New Testament passages that teach the wonderful truth of salvation through faith in Jesus Christ:

- "But as many as received him, to them gave he power to become the sons of God, even to them that believe on his name" (John 1:12 KJV).

- "And as Moses lifted up the bronze snake on a pole in the wilderness, so the Son of Man must be lifted up, so that everyone who believes in him will have eternal life" (John 3:14–15 NLT).

- "For God so loved the world, that he gave his only begotten Son, that whosoever believeth in him should not perish, but have everlasting life" (John 3:16 KJV).

- "Whoever believes in the Son has eternal life, but whoever rejects the Son will not see life, for God's wrath remains on them" (John 3:36 NIV).

- "Very truly I tell you, whoever hears my word and believes him who sent me has eternal life and will not be judged but has crossed over from death to life" (John 5:24 NIV).

- "Then they said to Him, 'What shall we do, that we may work the works of God?' Jesus answered and said to them, 'This is the work of God, that you believe in Him whom He sent'" (John 6:28–29 NKJV).

- "I am the resurrection and the life. He who believes in Me, though he may die, he shall live. And whoever lives and believes in Me shall never die" (John 11:25–26 NKJV).

- "Believe on the Lord Jesus Christ, and thou shalt be saved" (Acts 16:31 KJV).

- "Even the righteousness of God which is by faith of Jesus Christ unto all and upon all them that believe: for there is no difference" (Romans 3:22 KJV).

- "God presented Christ as a sacrifice of atonement, through the shedding of his blood—to be received by faith" (Romans 3:25 NIV).

- "He did it to demonstrate his righteousness at the present time, so as to be just and the one who justifies those who have faith in Jesus" (Romans 3:26 NIV).

- "For the Scriptures tell us, 'Abraham believed God, and God counted him as righteous because of his faith'" (Romans 4:3 NLT).

- "He [Abraham] received the sign of circumcision, a seal of the righteousness of the faith which he had while uncircumcised, so that he might be the father of all who believe without being circumcised, that righteousness might be credited to them" (Romans 4:11 NASB).

- "Therefore being justified by faith, we have peace with God through our Lord Jesus Christ: By whom also we have access by faith into this grace wherein we stand, and rejoice in hope of the glory of God" (Romans 5:1–2 KJV).

- "What shall we say then? That the Gentiles, which followed not after righteousness, have attained to righteousness, even the righteousness which is of faith" (Romans 9:30 KJV).

- "As it is written: 'See, I lay in Zion a stone that causes people to stumble and a rock that makes them fall, and the one who believes in him will never be put to shame'" (Romans 9:33 NIV).

- "If you confess with your mouth the Lord Jesus and believe in your heart that God has raised Him from the dead, you will be saved. For with the heart one believes unto righteousness, and with the mouth confession is made unto salvation" (Romans 10:9–10 NKJV).

- "For the Scripture says, 'Whoever believes on Him will not be put to shame'" (Romans 10:11 NKJV).

- "Scripture foresaw that God would justify the Gentiles by faith, and announced the gospel in advance to Abraham: 'All nations will be blessed through you.' So those who rely on faith are blessed along with Abraham, the man of faith" (Galatians 3:8–9 NIV).

- "He redeemed us in order that the blessing given to Abraham might come to the Gentiles through Christ Jesus, so that by faith we might receive the promise of the Spirit" (Galatians 3:14 NIV).

- "But Scripture has locked up everything under the control of sin, so that what was promised, being given through faith in Jesus Christ, might be given to those who believe" (Galatians 3:22 NIV).

- "In whom ye also trusted, after that ye heard the word of truth, the gospel of your salvation: in whom also after that ye believed, ye were sealed with that holy Spirit of promise" (Ephesians 1:13 KJV).

- "However, for this reason I obtained mercy, that in me first Jesus Christ might show all longsuffering, as a pattern to those who are going to believe on Him for everlasting life" (1 Timothy 1:16 NKJV).

- "Though you have not seen him, you love him; and even though you do not see him now, you believe in him and are filled with an inexpressible and glorious joy, for you are receiving the end result of your faith, the salvation of your souls" (1 Peter 1:8–9 NIV)

- "Whosoever believeth that Jesus is the Christ is born of God" (1 John 5:1 KJV).

- "And this is the testimony: God has given us eternal life, and this life is in his Son. Whoever has the Son has life; whoever does not have the Son of God does not have life. I write these things to you who believe in the name of the Son of God so that you may know that you have eternal life" (1 John 5:11–13 NIV).

Salvation by Faith. . .and Good Works?

The verses listed above should assure you that salvation comes to people *through faith in Jesus Christ alone*. There is nothing you can add to what Jesus has done on the cross—He has already done everything needed to pay for your sins and put you at peace with God.

The Westminster Shorter Catechism, a document written in question-and-answer format by English and Scottish religious leaders in the 1640s, nicely summarizes the above verses in question 86:

Q: What is faith in Jesus Christ?
A: Faith in Jesus Christ is a saving grace, whereby we receive and rest upon him alone for salvation, as he is offered to us in the gospel.

That seems simple enough, a message that echoes the words of Paul and Silas to the Philippian jailer. But there is a passage of scripture that—at least at first glance—seems to contradict the biblical teaching of salvation through faith alone. The apostle James penned these words that have confused some Christians over the centuries:

> *What good is it, my brothers and sisters, if someone claims to have faith but has no deeds? Can such faith save them? Suppose a brother or a sister is without clothes and daily food. If one of you says to them, "Go in peace; keep warm and well fed," but does nothing about their physical needs, what good is it? In the same way, faith by itself, if it is not accompanied by action, is dead.*
>
> JAMES 2:14–17 NIV

James muddies the water further when he goes on to write, "You see that a person is considered righteous by what they do and not by faith alone" (James 2:24 NIV).

These verses have been so troublesome that some argued that James's epistle shouldn't have been included in the Bible. And, on a quick reading, they do seem to be a direct contradiction to the many scriptures that say very clearly we are justified before God though faith alone. These verses insist we cannot be saved by any good deeds we do or by keeping the Law of Moses.

Here are some of those verses:

- "For we maintain that a person is justified by faith apart from the works of the law. Or is God the God of Jews only? Is he not the God of Gentiles too? Yes, of Gentiles too, since there is only one God, who will justify the circumcised by faith and the uncircumcised through that same faith" (Romans 3:28–30 NIV).

- "But people are counted as righteous, not because of their work, but because of their faith in God who forgives sinners" (Romans 4:5 NLT).

- "For this reason it is by faith, in order that it may be in accordance with grace, so that the promise will be guaranteed to all the descendants, not only to those who are of the Law, but also to those who are of the faith of Abraham, who is the father of us all" (Romans 4:16 NASB).

- "Christ is the culmination of the law so that there may be righteousness for everyone who believes" (Romans 10:4 NIV).

- "And if by grace, then it is no longer of works; otherwise grace is no longer grace. But if it is of works, it is no longer grace; otherwise work is no longer work" (Romans 11:6 NKJV).

- "Yet we know that a person is made right with God by faith in Jesus Christ, not by obeying the law. And we have believed in Christ Jesus, so that we might be made right with God because of our faith in Christ, not because we have obeyed the law. For no one will ever be made right with God by obeying the law" (Galatians 2:16 NLT).

- "I do not set aside the grace of God, for if righteousness could be gained through the law, Christ died for nothing!" (Galatians 2:21 NIV).

- "So again I ask, does God give you his Spirit and work miracles among you by the works of the law, or by your believing what you heard? So also Abraham 'believed God, and it was credited to him as righteousness'" (Galatians 3:5–6 NIV).

- "So the law was our guardian until Christ came that we might be justified by faith. Now that this faith has come, we are no longer under a guardian" (Galatians 3:24–25 NIV).

- "God saved you by his grace when you believed. And you can't take credit for this; it is a gift from God. Salvation is not a reward for the good things we have done, so none of us can boast about it" (Ephesians 2:8–9 NLT).

- ". . .be found in Him, not having my own righteousness, which is from the law, but that which is through faith in Christ, the righteousness which is from God by faith" (Philippians 3:9 NKJV).

So what about the words of the apostle James? He seems to say that no one can be saved unless they do good deeds. Did James miss a meeting when it was announced that salvation comes through faith alone? Was it a mistake to include his book in the Bible?

Actually, there is no contradiction at all between the writings of James and the many passages teaching salvation by faith in Christ alone. The verses you just read, indicating that salvation comes through faith in Christ alone, are the inspired Word of God—and so are the words of James. All of them are God's own words to us. They are absolute truth and you can depend on them.

James was merely pointing out that there will be a cause-and-effect process in the life of a person who has true faith in Jesus. In other words, if you have real faith in Christ, that faith will demonstrate itself in how you live, how you think, and how you treat others.

Jesus taught His disciples essentially the same thing in the parable of the sheep and the goats:

> *"Then the King will say to those on his right, 'Come, you who are blessed by my Father; take your inheritance, the kingdom prepared for you since the creation of the world. For I was hungry and you gave me something to eat, I was thirsty and you gave me something to drink, I was a stranger and you invited me in, I needed clothes and you clothed me, I was sick and you looked after me, I was in prison and you came to visit me.' Then the righteous will answer him, 'Lord, when did we see you hungry and feed you, or thirsty and give you something to drink? When did we see you a stranger and invite you in, or needing clothes and clothe you? When did we see you sick or in prison and go to visit you?' The*

King will reply, 'Truly I tell you, whatever you did for one of the least of these brothers and sisters of mine, you did for me.'"
MATTHEW 25:34–40 NIV

If you take this passage by itself, it seems Jesus is telling His followers that they would be saved through their acts of kindness—through giving the poor and needy housing, food, drink, and clothing. But if you look at this parable in the light of other scripture—including the words of Jesus Himself—you will see that *faith*, not acts of kindness and charity to others, leads to salvation.

Back to James: The apostle wanted his readers to understand the difference between a living, growing faith and a dead faith. The living faith shows itself through a changed life and good works—while a dead faith doesn't change anything. James 2:23 quotes Genesis 15:6 ("Abraham believed God, and it was credited to him as righteousness") and points out that Abraham proved his faith by obeying God's call to give up his own son.

The Bible is clear. Salvation comes through *faith* in Jesus Christ. Our salvation has nothing to do with our own merit or anything we've done. It has everything to do with God's compassion: "He saved us, not because of righteous things we had done, but because of his mercy" (Titus 3:5 NIV). But the Bible is also clear that "if anyone is in Christ, he is a new creation; old things have passed away; behold, all things have become new" (2 Corinthians 5:17 NKJV). This simply means that when we come to faith in Christ, we are saved *and* changed—changed in how we think, in how we behave, and in how we relate to other people. When we come to faith in Jesus, we turn from our old lives and old ways of thinking to an entirely new experience—including good works.

We are not saved *because* of our new thinking and good works; we engage in new thinking and good works because we are saved *through faith.*

The great nineteenth-century British preacher Charles Spurgeon summed it up well when he said, "Faith and works are bound up in the same bundle. He that obeys God trusts God; and he that trusts God obeys God. He that is without faith is without works; and he that is without works is without faith."

5

NEW TESTAMENT FAITH IN CHRIST

*I believe in Christianity as I believe that
the sun has risen: not only because I see it,
but because by it I see everything else.*
C.S. LEWIS

Living a life of faith will truly change the lives
of those who witness that faith in action. Jesus
was the perfect example of that.

The Gospels are filled with examples of
people who encountered Jesus and, moved by
what they experienced, came to life-changing
faith in Him. It started with His apostles, the
twelve men who would spend three-plus years

following Jesus closely, hearing Him teach, witnessing His miracles, and seeing Him complete the mission for which He came to earth—His sacrificial death on a cross.

Here are some incidents of faith in Jesus on the part of His twelve key followers:

- Peter and Andrew—"As Jesus was walking beside the Sea of Galilee, he saw two brothers, Simon called Peter and his brother Andrew. They were casting a net into the lake, for they were fishermen. 'Come, follow me,' Jesus said, 'and I will send you out to fish for people.' At once they left their nets and followed him" (Matthew 4:18–20 NIV).

- James and John—"Going on from there, he saw two other brothers, James son of Zebedee and his brother John. They were in a boat with their father Zebedee, preparing their nets. Jesus called them, and immediately they left the boat and their father and followed him" (Matthew 4:21–22 NIV).

- Philip—"The next day He purposed to go into Galilee, and He found Philip. And Jesus said to him, 'Follow Me.' Now Philip was from Bethsaida, of the city of Andrew and Peter. Philip found Nathanael and said to him, 'We have found Him of whom Moses in the Law and also the Prophets wrote—Jesus of Nazareth, the son of Joseph'" (John 1:43–45 NASB).

- Nathanael—"Jesus saw Nathanael coming to Him, and said of him, 'Behold, an Israelite indeed, in whom there is no deceit!' Nathanael said to Him, 'How do You know me?' Jesus answered and said to him, 'Before Philip called you, when you were under the fig tree, I saw you.' Nathanael answered Him, 'Rabbi, You are the Son of God; You are the King of Israel'" (John 1:47–49 NASB).

- The apostles at Cana—"This beginning of signs Jesus did in Cana of Galilee, and manifested His glory; and His disciples believed in Him" (John 2:11 NKJV).

- Peter—"Simon Peter answered and said, 'You are the Christ, the Son of the living God'" (Matthew 16:16 NKJV).

- The apostles as a group—"Now we are sure that You know all things, and have no need that anyone should question You. By this we believe that You came forth from God" (John 16:30 NKJV).

- John—"So the other disciple who had first come to the tomb then also entered, and he saw and believed" (John 20:8 NASB).

- Thomas—"And Thomas answered and said to Him, 'My Lord and my God!'" (John 20:28 NKJV).

In addition to the apostles, many other people who encountered Jesus responded to Him with faith. As you read through the following list, notice how these people's faith included some kind of action on their part—some came to Jesus, others brought friends to Him, still others had to ask for something, and so on:

- The Magi (wise men from the East)—"After Jesus was born in Bethlehem in Judea, during the time of King Herod, Magi from the east came to Jerusalem and asked, 'Where is the one who has been born king of the Jews? We saw his star when it rose and have come to worship him'. . . . On coming to the house, they saw the child with his mother Mary, and they bowed down and worshiped him. Then they opened their treasures and presented him with gifts of gold, frankincense and myrrh" (Matthew 2:1–2, 11 NIV).

- Mary, Jesus' mother, at the wedding at Cana—"When the wine ran out, the mother of Jesus said to Him, 'They have no wine.' And Jesus said to her, 'Woman, what does that have to do with us? My hour has not yet come.' His mother said to the servants, "Whatever He says to you, do it" (John 2:3–5 NASB).

- The Samaritans who heard the testimony of the woman at the well—"And many of the Samaritans of that city believed in Him because of the word of the woman who testified, 'He told me all that I ever did'" (John 4:39 NKJV).

- The woman with the issue of blood—"Just then a woman who had been subject to bleeding for twelve years came up behind him and touched the edge of his cloak. She said to herself, 'If I only touch his cloak, I will be healed.' Jesus turned and saw her. 'Take heart, daughter,' he said, 'your faith has healed you.' And the woman was healed at that moment" (Matthew 9:20–22 NIV).

- Jairus, the synagogue leader— "While [Jesus] was saying this, a synagogue leader came and knelt before him and said, 'My daughter has just died. But come and put your hand on her, and she will live.' . . . When Jesus entered the synagogue leader's house and saw the noisy crowd and people playing pipes, he said, 'Go away. The girl is not dead but asleep.' But they laughed at him. After the crowd had been put outside, he went in and took the girl by the hand, and she got up" (Matthew 9:18, 23–25 NIV).

- Two blind men—"As Jesus went on from there, two blind men followed him, calling out, 'Have mercy on us, Son of David!' When he had gone indoors, the blind men came to him, and he asked them, 'Do you believe that I am able to do this?' 'Yes, Lord,' they replied. Then he touched their eyes and said, 'According to your faith let it be done to you'; and their sight was restored" (Matthew 9:27–30 NIV).

- The father of a demon-possessed son—"A man in the crowd answered, 'Teacher, I brought you my son, who is possessed by a spirit that has robbed him of speech. Whenever it seizes him, it throws him to the ground. He foams at the mouth, gnashes his teeth and becomes rigid. . . . It has often thrown him into fire or water to kill him. But if you can do anything, take pity on us and help us.' "'If you can"?' said Jesus. 'Everything is possible for one who believes.' Immediately the boy's father exclaimed, 'I do believe; help me overcome my unbelief!' When Jesus saw that a crowd was running to the scene, he rebuked the impure spirit. 'You deaf and mute spirit,' he said, 'I command you, come out of him and never enter him again'" (Mark 9:17–18, 22–25 NIV).

- Blind Bartimaeus and blind companion—"And two blind men sitting by the road, hearing that Jesus was passing by, cried out, 'Lord, have mercy on us, Son of David!' The crowd sternly told them to be quiet, but they cried out all the more, 'Lord, Son of David, have mercy on us!' And Jesus stopped and called them, and said, 'What do you want Me to do for you?' They said to Him, 'Lord, we want our eyes to be opened.' Moved with compassion, Jesus touched their eyes; and immediately they regained their sight and followed Him" (Matthew 20:30–34 NASB; also see Mark 10:46–52, Luke 18:35–42).

- The Samaritan leper—"Now it happened as He went to Jerusalem that He passed through the midst of Samaria and Galilee. Then as He entered a certain village, there met Him ten men who were lepers, who stood afar off. And they lifted up their voices and said,

'Jesus, Master, have mercy on us!' So when He saw them, He said to them, 'Go, show yourselves to the priests.' And so it was that as they went, they were cleansed. And one of them, when he saw that he was healed, returned, and with a loud voice glorified God, and fell down on his face at His feet, giving Him thanks. And he was a Samaritan. So Jesus answered and said, 'Were there not ten cleansed? But where are the nine? Were there not any found who returned to give glory to God except this foreigner?' And He said to him, 'Arise, go your way. Your faith has made you well'" (Luke 17:11–19 NKJV).

- Sick people of Gennesaret—"When the people recognized Jesus, the news of his arrival spread quickly throughout the whole area, and soon people were bringing all their sick to be healed. They begged him to let the sick touch at least the fringe of his robe, and all who touched him were healed" (Matthew 14:35–36 NLT).

- Men who brought Jesus their paralyzed friend—"Some men came carrying a paralyzed man on a mat and tried to take him into the house to lay him before Jesus. When they could not find a way to do this because of the crowd, they went up on the roof and lowered him on his mat through the tiles into the middle of the crowd, right in front of Jesus. When Jesus saw their faith, he said, 'Friend, your sins are forgiven'" (Luke 5:18–20 NIV).

- The Syrophoenician woman—"In fact, as soon as she heard about him, a woman whose little daughter was possessed by an impure spirit came and fell at his feet. The woman was a Greek, born in Syrian Phoenicia. She begged Jesus to drive the demon out of her daughter. 'First let the children eat all they want,' he told her, 'for it is not right to take the children's bread and toss it to the dogs.' 'Lord,' she replied, 'even the dogs under the table eat the children's crumbs.'

Then he told her, 'For such a reply, you may go; the demon has left your daughter.' She went home and found her child lying on the bed, and the demon gone" (Mark 7:25–30 NIV; also see Matthew 15:22–28).

- The woman who anointed Jesus' feet—"When one of the Pharisees invited Jesus to have dinner with him, he went to the Pharisee's house and reclined at the table. A woman in that town who lived a sinful life learned that Jesus was eating at the Pharisee's house, so she came there with an alabaster jar of perfume. As she stood behind him at his feet weeping, she began to wet his feet with her tears. Then she wiped them with her hair, kissed them and poured perfume on them" (Luke 7:36–38 NIV).

- Those who brought those who were sick with palsy—"And, behold, they brought to him a man sick of the palsy, lying on a bed: and Jesus seeing their faith said unto the sick of the palsy; Son, be of good cheer; thy sins be forgiven thee" (Matthew 9:2 KJV).

- The nobleman whose child was sick—"So Jesus came again to Cana of Galilee where He had made the water wine. And there was a certain nobleman whose son was sick at Capernaum. When he heard that Jesus had come out of Judea into Galilee, he went to Him and implored Him to come down and heal his son, for he was at the point of death. Then Jesus said to him, 'Unless you people see signs and wonders, you will by no means believe.' The nobleman said to Him, 'Sir, come down before my child dies!' Jesus said to him, 'Go your way; your son lives.' So the man believed the word that Jesus spoke to him, and he went his way. And as he was now going down, his servants met him and told him, saying, 'Your son lives!' Then he inquired of them the hour when he got better. And they said to him,

'Yesterday at the seventh hour the fever left him.' So the father knew that it was at the same hour in which Jesus said to him, 'Your son lives.' And he himself believed, and his whole household" (John 4:46–53 NKJV).

- The blind man Jesus healed on the Sabbath—"Then [Jesus] spit on the ground, made mud with the saliva, and spread the mud over the blind man's eyes. He told him, 'Go wash yourself in the pool of Siloam' (Siloam means 'sent'). So the man went and washed and came back seeing! . . . When Jesus heard what had happened, he found the man and asked, 'Do you believe in the Son of Man?' The man answered, 'Who is he, sir? I want to believe in him.' 'You have seen him,' Jesus said, 'and he is speaking to you!' 'Yes, Lord, I believe!' the man said. And he worshiped Jesus" (John 9:6–7, 35–38 NLT).

- Mary, the sister of Martha—"As Jesus and the disciples continued on their way to Jerusalem, they came to a certain village where a woman named Martha welcomed him into her home. Her sister, Mary, sat at the Lord's feet, listening to what he taught. But Martha was distracted by the big dinner she was preparing. She came to Jesus and said, 'Lord, doesn't it seem unfair to you that my sister just sits here while I do all the work? Tell her to come and help me.' But the Lord said to her, 'My dear Martha, you are worried and upset over all these details! There is only one thing worth being concerned about. Mary has discovered it, and it will not be taken away from her'" (Luke 10:38–42 NLT).

More New Testament Faith in Christ

Many people, after personally witnessing or learning of the miraculous works and powerful teaching of Jesus Christ, responded to Him in faith during His earthly ministry. But that was just the beginning. The New Testament reports that after Jesus' death and resurrection, the preaching of powerful men of faith—such as the apostles Peter, John, and Paul—led to literally thousands of people coming to the faith.

Here is a list of many of those New Testament-era converts:

- About 3,000 people in Jerusalem on the day of Pentecost—"Those who accepted his message were baptized, and about three thousand were added to their number that day" (Acts 2:41 NIV).

- More than 5,000 people in Jerusalem—"But many of the people who heard their message believed it, so the number of believers now totaled about 5,000 men, not counting women and children" (Acts 4:4 NLT).

- Unnamed multitudes—"And all the more believers in the Lord, multitudes of men and women, were constantly added to their number" (Acts 5:14 NASB).

- The crippled man at Lystra—"And in Lystra a certain man without strength in his feet was sitting, a cripple from his mother's womb, who had never walked. This man heard Paul speaking. Paul, observing him intently and seeing that he had faith to be healed, said with a loud voice, 'Stand up straight on your feet!' And he leaped and walked" (Acts 14:8–10 NKJV).

- Stephen—"And Stephen, full of faith and power, did great wonders and miracles among the people" (Acts 6:8 KJV).

- The Ethiopian eunuch—"And Philip said, 'If you believe with all your heart, you may.' And he answered and said, 'I believe that Jesus Christ is the Son of God'" (Acts 8:37 NASB).

- Aeneas—"Peter said to him, 'Aeneas, Jesus Christ heals you; get up and make your bed.' Immediately he got up" (Acts 9:34 NASB).

- The people of Lydda and Sharon—"All those who lived in Lydda and Sharon saw him and turned to the Lord" (Acts 9:35 NIV).

- The people of Joppa—"This became known all over Joppa, and many people believed in the Lord" (Acts 9:42 NIV).

- The people of Antioch—"Some of them, however, men from Cyprus and Cyrene, went to Antioch and began to speak to Greeks also, telling them the good news about the Lord Jesus. The Lord's hand was with them, and a great number of people believed and turned to the Lord. . . . He was a good man, full of the Holy Spirit and faith, and a great number of people were brought to the Lord" (Acts 11:20–21, 24 NIV).

- Sergius Paulus—"When the proconsul saw what had happened, he believed, for he was amazed at the teaching about the Lord" (Acts 13:12 NIV).

- Eunice, Lois, and Timothy—"Then he came to Derbe and Lystra. And behold, a certain disciple was there, named Timothy, the son of a certain Jewish woman who believed, but his father *was* Greek" (Acts 16:1 NKJV).

- Lydia—"Now a certain woman named Lydia heard us. She was a seller of purple from the city of Thyatira, who worshiped God. The Lord opened her heart to heed the things spoken by Paul" (Acts 16:14 NKJV).

- The Philippian jailer and his family—"They replied, 'Believe in the Lord Jesus and you will be saved, along with everyone in your household.' And they shared the word of the Lord with him and with all who lived in his household. Even at that hour of the night, the jailer cared for them and washed their wounds. Then he and everyone in his household were immediately baptized. He brought them into his house and set a meal before them, and he and his entire household rejoiced because they all believed in God" (Acts 16:31–34 NLT).

- Crispus and others in Corinth— "Crispus, the leader of the synagogue, and everyone in his household believed in the Lord. Many others in Corinth also heard Paul, became believers, and were baptized" (Acts 18:8 NLT).

- Jews at Rome—"And when they had appointed him a day, there came many to him into his lodging; to whom he expounded and testified the kingdom of God, persuading them concerning Jesus, both out of the law of Moses, and out of the prophets, from morning till evening. And some believed the things which were spoken, and some believed not" (Acts 28:23–24 KJV).

- The Ephesians—"In Him, you also, after listening to the message of truth, the gospel of your salvation—having also believed, you were sealed in Him with the Holy Spirit of promise, who is given as a pledge of our inheritance, with a view to the redemption of God's own possession, to the praise of His glory" (Ephesians 1:13–14 NASB).

- The Colossians—"To the saints and faithful brethren in Christ who are at Colossae: Grace to you and peace from God our Father. We give thanks to God, the Father of our Lord Jesus Christ, praying always for you, since we heard of your faith in Christ Jesus and the love which you have for all the saints" (Colossians 1:2–4 NASB).

- The Thessalonians—"You became imitators of us and of the Lord, for you welcomed the message in the midst of severe suffering with the joy given by the Holy Spirit" (1 Thessalonians 1:6 NIV).

- Philemon—"I always thank my God as I remember you in my prayers, because I hear about your love for all his holy people and your faith in the Lord Jesus" (Philemon 4–5 NIV).

The way Christianity spread through the first century demonstrates a wonderful truth about faith: It is, in many ways, contagious. Because just a few people courageously lived lives of faith, many other lives—and eternal destinations—were changed.

6

ENCOURAGEMENT FROM
THE FAITH HALL OF FAME

Expect great things from God.
Attempt great things for God.
WILLIAM CAREY

Ever feel discouraged in your faith, in need
of a little pick-me-up? Then open your Bible
to the New Testament's book of Hebrews
and thumb your way to chapter 11. There,
in what has been called the "Hall of Faith"
or the "Faith Hall of Fame," you'll find encouragement and motivation to move forward
in your life of faith.

The people listed in this chapter weren't

perfect. While a few of them walked consistent lives of faith and obedience (Samuel, for example), most of them were flawed human beings who made some poor, even terrible, decisions. Noah got drunk (Genesis 9:21–22), Abraham lied (Genesis 12:10–20, 20:2), Jacob cheated and manipulated to get what he wanted (Genesis 27), Moses doubted his own ability to lead (Exodus 3–4) and in the end lost both his cool and his place in the Promised Land (Numbers 20:1–13). Rahab was a prostitute (Joshua 2:1), and Samson failed due to his lust and bad temper (Judges 13–16). Then there was David. . . Where do we start? David committed adultery and murder (2 Samuel 11:1–27) and more than once allowed his temper to get the best of him (see 1 Samuel 25). Talk about a flawed hero of the faith!

Still, Hebrews 11 serves as a source of comfort and encouragement for the believer who wants to live a life of faith in God. Here is a brief look at the people whose contributions to the kingdom of God earned them a place in the Faith Hall of Fame:

- Abel—"By faith Abel brought God a better offering than Cain did. By faith he was commended as righteous, when God spoke well of his offerings. And by faith Abel still speaks, even though he is dead" (Hebrews 11:4 NIV).

The Bible doesn't tell us a lot about Abel, other than that he was Adam and Eve's second son and worked as a shepherd. The writer of Hebrews tells us that Abel was a man of faith who brought God a pleasing sacrifice of "fat portions from some of the firstborn of his flock" (Genesis 4:4 NIV). Cain, Abel's older brother, was a farmer who brought some of the fruits of his labor to God as a sacrifice—but for reasons that have been debated for centuries, his sacrifice did not please God. This sent Cain into a fit of rage, and he made Abel the first victim of murder and the first martyr in human history. You can read the whole story in Genesis 4:1–15.

- Enoch—"By faith Enoch was taken from this life, so that he did not experience death: 'He could not be found, because God had taken him away.' For before he was taken, he was commended as one who pleased God. And without faith it is impossible to please God, because anyone who comes to him must believe that he exists and that he rewards those who earnestly seek him" (Hebrews 11:5–6 NIV).

Unlike most of the other faith heroes named in Hebrews 11, nothing is recorded of Enoch's exploits as a follower of God. He is simply described as a man who "walked with God." Everything we know about his life is recorded in seven short verses in the fifth chapter of the Genesis. This passage (Genesis 5:18–24) tells us that his father was a man named Jared, that he was Methuselah's father, that he lived 365 years and fathered other sons and daughters, and that he walked faithfully with God for three hundred years. Finally, it tells us that after those three hundred years, "he was no more, because God took him away" (Genesis 5:24 NIV). The writer of Hebrews implies that Enoch never died because God took him straight to heaven.

- Noah——"By faith Noah, being divinely warned of things not yet seen, moved with godly fear, prepared an ark for the saving of his household, by which he condemned the world and became heir of the righteousness which is according to faith" (Hebrews 11:7 NKJV).

Noah was a righteous man who walked with God at a time when wickedness had overtaken all humankind. The earth was hopelessly lost in sin and violence, and a grieving God had decided to destroy the world He'd created and start over. God knew Noah was the only man with the faith to believe Him and follow His instructions for building the ark. That would be home for Noah, his family, and the creatures of the earth until the floodwaters subsided.

As you read Noah's story in Genesis 6–9, you'll see that he was not a perfect man. But Noah was a man whose faith and obedience were just what was needed to ensure that his family would be saved. Though Noah's faith, humankind would survive for generations to come.

- Abraham—"It was by faith that Abraham obeyed when God called him to leave home and go to another land that God would give him as his inheritance. He went without knowing where he was going. And even when he reached the land God promised him, he lived there by faith—for he was like a foreigner, living in tents. And so did Isaac and Jacob, who inherited the same promise. Abraham was confidently looking forward to a city with eternal foundations, a city designed and built by God" (Hebrews 11:8–10 NLT; also see verses 12–19).

No single member of the Bible's

Faith Hall of Fame receives more attention than Abraham, father of the Jewish nation and of the Christian faith. Abraham was an amazing example of what it means, as the apostle Paul put it, to walk by faith and not by sight (see 2 Corinthians 5:7). You can read Abraham's fascinating story in Genesis 12–25.

The writer of Hebrews lauds Abraham's willingness to obey God—to leave his home in Haran and head to a place he didn't know, simply because God told him to do it (see Genesis 12:1–4). Abraham (then called Abram) didn't question or doubt God. We have no record of him asking God where he would end up; he simply believed the Lord and His promises and hit the road.

While Abraham was far from perfect, his life was marked by faith in God—and by the kind of obedience faith always brings. An almost unbelievable example of this faith-obedience walk came later in Abraham's life, when God commanded him to offer up his long-awaited son Isaac as a sacrifice: "Take your son, your only son, whom you love—Isaac—and go to the region of Moriah. Sacrifice him there as a burnt offering on a mountain I will show you" (Genesis 22:2 NIV).

The Bible doesn't tell Abraham's thoughts of this shocking commandment. But it says he arose the next morning, loaded his donkey with enough wood for a burnt offering, and headed to Moriah with two servants and his beloved son. Abraham was fully prepared to sacrifice Isaac; in fact, he was just a moment away from ending the young man's life when the angel of the Lord stopped him. "Do not lay a hand on the boy," the angel said. "Do not do anything to him. Now I know that you fear God, because you have not withheld from me your son, your only son" (Genesis 22:12 NIV).

We might consider these acts of obedience on Abraham's part as nothing more than blind faith—but they were anything but that. Abraham had such belief and trust in God that he was willing to do everything He commanded, exactly as He commanded—even when those commands made no earthly sense. Even when they required him to surrender a precious thing God had miraculously given him—his own son.

That's why Abraham is mentioned so prominently in Hebrews 11. It's why he played such an important part in God's plan for establishing His chosen people, the Israelites, and for bringing salvation to the whole world.

- Sarah—"And by faith even Sarah, who was past childbearing age, was enabled to bear children because she considered him faithful who had made the promise" (Hebrews 11:11 NIV).

  Abraham's wife, Sarah, is an example of timing—of the fact that faith doesn't always bring about the fulfillment of God's promises when we think it should. In fact, Sarah shows that we may have to wait on God, sometimes for a long time, before He does what He's said He will do.

Sarah's example also shows that God doesn't always fulfill His promises in the ways we expect. That was certainly true in the birth of Isaac.

At times, Sarah doubted that God would fulfill His promise to give her a son. After waiting many years without becoming pregnant, Sarah persuaded Abraham to sleep with her servant Hagar so that he could produce an heir. The plan resulted in a son named Ishmael.

But Ishmael was not the heir God had promised Abraham. God reassured Abraham that, even though Sarah was well past the usual childbearing years, his wife would bear him a son: "Is anything too hard for the LORD? At the appointed time I will return to you, according to the time of life, and Sarah shall have a son" (Genesis 18:14 NKJV).

When the time was right, God fulfilled His promise. Sarah became pregnant with a son. Abraham was a century old when Isaac, the child of promise, was born.

Sarah wasn't perfect in her faith—she even laughed when she heard that she would become pregnant at her age (Genesis 18:12–15). She believed God's promises—but also felt she had to take matters into her own hands to bring about their fulfillment. Still, Sarah's obedience to God earned her a place in the Faith Hall of Fame—and provides us an example of how God sometimes fulfills His promises through the miraculous.

- Isaac—"By faith Isaac blessed Jacob and Esau in regard to their future" (Hebrews 11:20 NIV).

  Like his father Abraham, the Jewish patriarch Isaac was an imperfect man who nonetheless is mentioned in the New Testament Faith Hall of Fame. Also like Abraham, Isaac married a woman who was unable to have children—at least without help from the Lord. Being a man of faith as well as a devoted husband, Isaac prayed for Rebekah, and eventually God allowed her to conceive and carry twins: Esau and Jacob (Genesis 25:21–26).

* Jacob—"By faith Jacob, when he was dying, blessed each of Joseph's sons, and worshiped as he leaned on the top of his staff" (Hebrews 11:21 NIV).

Jacob, Esau's twin brother, was the great patriarch of Israel who fathered twelve sons. They became heads of the nation's twelve "tribes." But Jacob was no paragon of faith and obedience to God. Early on, he lied, deceived, cheated, and manipulated his way into taking a blessing that rightfully belonged to his brother.

Jacob's life, however, took a dramatic turn after an all-night wrestling match. . . with God Himself! The tussle ended with God touching Jacob's hip, dislocating it. From that point forward, Jacob went through life with a limp and a new name: Israel, meaning "he struggles with God." Jacob was a new man with a new purpose, namely trust in and dependence on his God.

Jacob serves as an example of how God can take a deeply imperfect man and use him to bless many other people. You can read his complete story in Genesis 25–49.

- Joseph—"By faith Joseph, when his end was near, spoke about the exodus of the Israelites from Egypt and gave instructions concerning the burial of his bones" (Hebrews 11:22 NIV).

Besides Moses, Joseph is probably the greatest example of faith in the entire Old Testament. No matter what happened to Joseph—and he suffered more than his share of injustice—he trusted God completely. Joseph always believed that God would bring something good out of the worst situations.

Joseph is a great hero of the faith,

but even he had his flaws. As a youth, Joseph came across as arrogant, flaunting his status as Jacob's favorite son before his brothers. They were so angry with Joseph that they threw him down a dry well, then sold him as a slave to passing travelers. That was only after they decided not to kill him because he was more valuable financially alive than dead.

The caravan carted Joseph off to Egypt, where he was again sold to an official named Potiphar. Joseph never complained about his treatment. Instead, he worked so hard that he was assigned a high position in Potiphar's estate. Then he suffered another reverse: Potiphar's wife, who had unsuccessfully tried to seduce Joseph, falsely accused him of attempted rape. Potiphar had Joseph thrown into prison.

Even at that, we have no record of Joseph questioning why God would allow such injustice. Eventually, through a miraculous chain of events, Joseph became a key official in Egypt, leading the nation through a terrible famine and saving his own family from starvation.

Joseph's faith in God allowed him to extend real, heartfelt forgiveness to his brothers for the wrong they had done to him. When he was finally reunited with his brothers, who had come to Egypt hoping to find food, he spoke from his heart: "You intended to harm me, but God intended it all for good. He brought me to this position so I could save the lives of many people" (Genesis 50:20 NLT).

You can read Joseph's story in Genesis 30–50.

- Amram and Jochebed (Moses' parents)—"By faith Moses' parents hid him for three months after he was born, because they saw he was no ordinary child, and they were not afraid of the king's edict" (Hebrews 11:23 NIV).

While the writer of Hebrews doesn't mention Moses' parents by name, they are nonetheless important figures in the

Old Testament—and amazing pictures of steadfast faith in their God.

The story of Moses' birth is found in Exodus 2, which also doesn't mention his parents by name. (You'll find them specified in Exodus 6:20.) Moses was born in Egypt at a time when Pharaoh, fearful of the ever-expanding population of Hebrews in his country, had decreed that all male newborns should be killed.

For hiding the baby Moses, the Faith Hall of Fame acclaims Moses' parents for their lack of fear toward Pharaoh and for their faith in God. Their obedience ensured that one day Moses could lead the Hebrews out of Egyptian captivity and slavery.

- Moses—"By faith Moses, when he had grown up, refused to be known as the son of Pharaoh's daughter. He chose to be mistreated along with the people of God rather than to enjoy the fleeting pleasures of sin. He regarded disgrace for the sake of Christ as of greater value than the treasures of Egypt, because he was looking ahead to his reward. By faith he left Egypt, not fearing the king's anger; he persevered because he saw him who is invisible. By faith he kept the Passover and the application of blood, so that the destroyer of the firstborn would not touch the firstborn of Israel" (Hebrews 11:24–28 NIV).

Moses, like Abraham, is mentioned prominently in Hebrews 11. Like so many Bible characters, Moses had weaknesses. He feared, he doubted, and he lost his temper. Yet he stands as an enduring example of faith, and that in the face of incredible opposition—from both the worldly powers of his time and, eventually, from his own people.

Though Moses saw himself as unworthy of the call God had for him (see Exodus 3–4), he still led his people with courage and conviction. Moses stood up to Pharaoh, the most powerful man in the most powerful nation in the world at that time, then led the Hebrew people out of Egypt. Moses received the Law from God Himself and delivered it to the people, then led them to the edge of the Promised Land. Along the way, Moses recorded the first five books of the Hebrew Bible, also known as the Pentateuch: Genesis, Exodus, Leviticus, Numbers, and Deuteronomy.

Moses shows how God can use even the unworthy to accomplish His purposes—as long as they act in faith. Moses didn't believe in himself—at least at first—but he believed in God and in His promises. That was enough to earn Moses a prominent place in the Faith Hall of Fame.

- The Hebrews of the Exodus—"By faith the people passed through the Red Sea as on dry land; but when the Egyptians tried to do so, they were drowned" (Hebrews 11:29 NIV).

As you read the story of the Exodus and the events that followed, you'll see that the people of Israel were often an unruly lot. They were ungrateful, rebellious, and faithless—in fact, at one point they wanted to return to slavery in Egypt rather than take possession of the Promised Land!

But Hebrews 11 put them—an estimated two or three million in number—in the Faith Hall of Fame simply because they had the faith-inspired courage to cross the Red Sea "as on dry land." When Egyptian soldiers who did not have faith in God tried to follow them, they drowned in the sea.

- Israel's Army—"By faith the walls of Jericho fell, after the army had marched around them for seven days" (Hebrews 11:30 NIV).

  While no specific Old Testament character is named in Hebrews 11:30, this verse refers to the Israelite army's conquest of the mighty city of Jericho—which they accomplished through rather unconventional means. God had instructed Joshua, the army commander and Moses' successor as leader of the Israelites, to have his army march around Jericho for six days straight. On the seventh day, they were to circle the city seven times, followed by blasts on trumpets by seven Hebrew priests. When the army did as God had commanded, Jericho's walls collapsed and the Israelites took possession of the city (see Joshua 6).

Joshua was a man of uncompromising faith. When God gave him instructions for the conquest of Jericho, he followed them to the very last detail— even though the plan made little human sense.

- Rahab—"By faith the prostitute Rahab, because she welcomed the spies, was not killed with those who were disobedient" (Hebrews 11:31 NIV).

Humanly speaking, Rahab, one of two women mentioned by name in the Faith Hall of Fame, would seem least likely candidate for inclusion. Rahab worked as a prostitute in the city of Jericho. But when two Israelite spies arrived in her hometown, she hid them from the king of Jericho, risking her own life to save theirs.

Rahab recognized the God of the Israelites as the true, living God. After lying to the king's soldiers about where the Israelites had gone, she approached the spies and pleaded for her life and the lives of her family members. When the city of Jericho fell, Rahab and her family were spared and taken into the community of the Hebrews.

Because of her newfound faith, Rahab not only survived the fall of Jericho but was listed as an ancestor of both King David and Jesus Christ (see Matthew 1:5) and as a member of the New Testament's Faith Hall of Fame.

The lesson we take from the life of Rahab is that it's faith, not our background, that determines whether God can do great things in and through us. You can read Rahab's story in Joshua 2 and 6.

Other Faith Hall-of-Famers

The writer of Hebrews acknowledges that he didn't have the time to recount the lives and exploits of every Old Testament hero or heroine of the faith. So he closes this incredible passage like this:

And what more shall I say? For time will fail me if I tell of Gideon, Barak, Samson, Jephthah, of David and Samuel and the prophets, who by faith conquered kingdoms, performed acts of righteousness, obtained promises, shut the mouths of lions, quenched the power of fire, escaped the edge of the sword, from weakness were made strong, became mighty in war, put foreign armies to flight. Women received back their dead by resurrection; and others were tortured, not accepting their release, so that they might obtain a better resurrection; and others experienced mockings and scourgings, yes, also chains and imprisonment. They were stoned, they were sawn in two, they were tempted, they

were put to death with the sword; they
went about in sheepskins, in goatskins,
being destitute, afflicted, ill-treated (men
of whom the world was not worthy),
wandering in deserts and mountains and
caves and holes in the ground.
HEBREWS 11:32–38 NASB

- Gideon (verse 32)—Like many
amazing men of faith listed in scripture,
Gideon was a flawed man. He was one
of the dozen or so judges of Israel (the
judges led the people before the nation
became a monarchy), and he served
his God and nation brilliantly. At the
same time, he knew his weaknesses
and battled through times of doubt. In
spite of Gideon's slowness to believe,
in spite of his own self-doubt, he
became convinced of God's power to
do great things through him. That faith
allowed him to become one of the great
members of the Faith Hall of Fame. You
can read his story in Judges 6–8.

- Barak (verse 32)—Barak was an Israelite warrior who courageously stood up to the Canaanite army despite overwhelming odds. Like many others included in the Hall of Faith, Barak had his moments of weakness. When Deborah (the only woman among Israel's judges) called on Barak to go to Mount Tabor to battle King Jabin's Canaanite army, he hesitated, telling Deborah he would go only if she went with him. Because of this weakness, he didn't receive credit for the victory over the Canaanites. Still, he had enough faith to be included in the New Testament's Hall of Faith. You can read his story in Judges 4–5.

- Samson (verse 32)—The Old Testament portrays Samson as a man of incredible potential and strength but also as a man who wasted his many gifts on sinful living and on trying to accomplish great things through his own strength. He fought bravely, even slaying 1,000 Philistines using the jawbone of a donkey as his weapon. Still, in the end, Samson failed to consistently walk in a life of faith. Amazingly, however, he is listed in the Hall of Faith. In the end, Samson was humbled and returned to God—the One who was the source of all his strength all along. Samson's story appears in Judges 13–16.

- Jephthah (verse 32)—Another of Israel's judges, Jephthah was a courageous warrior and an outstanding military leader. He accomplished great things for his nation when he trusted God—but he also made a rash decision that resulted in disaster for his family. You can read Jephthah's story in Judges 11–12.

- David (verse 32)—The life of Israel's second and greatest monarch is featured in detail in the Old Testament but receives only a quick mention in Hebrews 11. David is remembered as the one who had the faith and courage to face and kill a giant Philistine named Goliath. David is known as a courageous military leader and a great king. He also wrote more than half of the Old Testament book of Psalms.

As mentioned earlier in this chapter, David was a deeply flawed man—and he's depicted that way in Old Testament scripture (the story of his sin with Bathsheba and the deadly cover-up that followed is recounted in detail in 2 Samuel 11–12). Yet David was called "a man after [God's] own heart" (1 Samuel 13:14 NIV). Why? Because David didn't focus on his own qualities but on those of His God. David failed in many ways, but he still lived a life of deep faith in the goodness and mercy of his God.

- Samuel (verse 32)—Of all the people listed in the Faith Hall of Fame, Samuel stands out as a man who served God with great loyalty and with unshakable, unwavering faith. While others around him turned from God and made disastrous decisions, Samuel continued to walk a life of integrity and faith. Through this obedience to God, he earned his place as a hero of the faith. You can read his story in the Book of 1 Samuel.

- Unnamed Faith Hall-of-Famers (verses 33–38)—The Faith Hall of Fame closes with a list of unnamed heroes of the faith. While we don't see their names listed, the things they did are briefly spelled out, giving us a good idea of their identity. Verse 33 tells us that one hero of the faith, "shut the mouth of lions" (NIV). This most likely refers to the prophet Daniel, who was thrown into a lions' den but came out unharmed (see Daniel 6:10–23).

The writer of Hebrews probably drew from the book of Daniel again (3:19–25) when he wrote that certain heroes of the faith "quenched the power of fire" (Hebrews 11:34 NASB). This

most likely refers to Daniel's friends—
Shadrach, Meshach, and Abednego—
who were thrown into a blazing hot
furnace but came out of the ordeal
without even minor injuries.

In verse 34, the writer of Hebrews
wrote of those "became mighty in war,
put foreign armies to flight." This can
refer to any of several great warriors
we read about in the Old Testament—
David, Joshua, Barak, and others.

Verse 35 ("Women received back
their dead, raised to life again") could
refer to the widow of Zarephath (see
1 Kings 17:17–24) and the Shunammite
woman (see 2 Kings 4:8–37), whose
sons were both raised from the dead
through the faith of the prophets Elijah
and Elisha, respectively.

Verses 35–36 say, "others were
tortured, not accepting their release,
so that they might obtain a better
resurrection; and others experienced
mockings and scourgings, yes, also

chains and imprisonment." This passage echoes Matthew 5:12, in which Jesus referred to the persecution Old Testament prophets experienced for speaking the truth. One of the greatest prophets, Jeremiah, fits this description almost perfectly: Because he spoke out so faithfully and forcefully, he was whipped and placed in stocks by the authorities of his time (see Jeremiah 20).

And verse 37 tells us that some of these heroes of the faith "were stoned," that some were "sawn in two," and others were "put to death with the sword." The Old Testament reports that Zechariah, high priest during the times of Kings Ahaziah and Joash, was stoned to death after speaking out against the king and the people over their rebellion against God (see 2 Chronicles 24:21). The hero of the faith who was "sawn in two" could be the prophet Isaiah. While the Bible doesn't tell us how Isaiah died, ancient Jewish tradition holds that he was placed in a hollowed out tree and cut in two.

Lessons from the Faith Hall of Fame

The Faith Hall of Fame is an inspiring collection of stories of Old Testament men and women. It can both encourage and challenge us to live lives of faith.

This important passage teaches us many lessons about what faith really is and what it means to walk in faith. Two of those lessons stand out:

First, the faith life is not about us, and it never has been! God has always used imperfect people to do amazing things. Why? Because God wants us to understand that this life of faith is not about what we can do for Him—rather, it's about what He can do in and through us. Our own imperfections serve as reminders that we need a faith that makes us completely dependent upon God to do in us, through us, and for us what we can't do ourselves.

Second, faith doesn't equal ease. Many of Faith Hall of Famers had to endure hardships and suffering. And we see that theme throughout the Bible. In the Old and New

Testaments alike, we read of people of faith enduring all sorts of suffering. These accounts serve as a reminder that while God *has* promised us ultimate victory through Jesus Christ, He *hasn't* promised us that life would be easy. In fact, scripture promises exactly the opposite.

It is quite safe to say that your faith will at some point be tested—tested by the world, tested by people around you, even tested by the devil himself. But the Bible promises that those tests are for your own good and that you will emerge from them stronger and more grounded in your faith. As the apostle Peter wrote, God uses the trials you face to test your faith, to show that it is strong and pure. "It is being tested as fire tests and purifies gold—though your faith is far more precious than mere gold. So when your faith remains strong through many trials, it will bring you much praise and glory and honor on the day when Jesus Christ is revealed to the whole world" (1 Peter 1:7 NLT).

7

GROWING YOUR FAITH

The principle part of faith is patience.
GEORGE MACDONALD

It's been rightly said that you can't stay in one place in your life of faith: You're either moving forward or falling backward.

If you've been a Christian for any amount of time, you should be able to look back and see that your faith—in spite of momentary failures—has grown stronger, making you more and more like Jesus as time has gone on.

When you first came to believe in Jesus Christ as Lord and Savior, you were the spiritual equivalent of a newborn. But just as an infant who receives nourishment from his mother begins the process of growing—from infancy to toddlerhood, from toddlerhood to school age, from school age to adolescence, and from adolescence to adulthood—the nourishment you receive from your Father will, over time, grow you spiritually, too. Ultimately, you'll become the man or woman of God He intends you to be.

Sounds great, doesn't it? But it's important to understand that this growth doesn't "just happen." If you want to grow stronger and more mature in your faith, you'll have to put some spiritual "elbow grease" into the process. Just as a child's physical growth depends on taking in his parents' provision, your growth in the faith life requires a certain effort. It starts with spending time reading and studying the ultimate Book of faith, the Bible.

Time in the Word of God

The great nineteenth-century American evangelist Dwight L. Moody had a lot to say about the central role of faith in the Christian life. One of the most powerful—if not *the* most powerful—things Moody ever said on the subject was his testimony as to the importance of learning what God Himself had to say about true faith:

> *I prayed for faith and thought that someday faith would come down and strike me like lightning. But faith did not seem to come. One day I read in the tenth chapter of Romans, "Faith cometh by hearing, and hearing by the Word of God." I had up to this time closed my Bible and prayed for faith. I now opened my Bible and began to study, and faith has been growing ever since.*

A simple and powerful truth from an amazing man of faith!

Certainly, Moody wasn't minimizing the importance of prayer as an element of a believer's growing and strengthening faith. He was, as much as anything, a man of prayer. But Moody understood that time in prayer and time in God's Word are equally important in the life of the believer who wants faith to grow. You could say that one won't work without the other.

The Bible has much to say about the Word of God's power to grow a believer's faith. Here are just a few examples, including the verse Moody cited in the above quotation:

- "Jesus answered, 'It is written: "Man shall not live on bread alone, but on every word that comes from the mouth of God"'" (Matthew 4:4 NIV).

- "So then faith cometh by hearing, and hearing by the word of God" (Romans 10:17 KJV).

- "Like newborn babies, crave pure spiritual milk, so that by it you may grow up in your salvation" (1 Peter 2:2 NIV).

- "All Scripture is God-breathed and is useful for teaching, rebuking, correcting and training in righteousness, so that the servant of God may be thoroughly equipped for every good work" (2 Timothy 3:16–17 NIV).

- "For the word of God is alive and active. Sharper than any double-edged sword, it penetrates even to dividing soul and spirit, joints and marrow; it judges the thoughts and attitudes of the heart" (Hebrews 4:12 NIV).

The Bible is all about growth in your faith. Not only will you discover instruction, you'll find encouragement as you see the exploits of people who have lived amazing lives of faith.

If you want to strengthen and grow your faith, make sure you spend time in the Word of God. Read it, study it, and memorize it. Do these things on your own and in group settings. Meditate on the direction God has provided for growing your faith beyond what you could ever imagine.

Talking to the Author and Finisher of Your Faith—Daily!

Think back for a moment to Dwight L. Moody. He stated that he had spent a lot of time praying for more faith, only to be met with silence. When he began reading his Bible more regularly, his faith grew bigger and stronger, allowing him to accomplish stunning things for the kingdom of God.

Now here's a question: Do you think Moody *stopped* praying once he started reading his Bible more regularly? Absolutely not! You don't accomplish the things D. L. Moody did without spending a lot of time in prayer.

Bible reading and prayer are the twin foundations of a growing faith. When we do *our* part—regularly reading the Bible and praying—God does *His* part in strengthening and growing our faith.

This idea of God responding to our prayerful requests to strengthen our faith isn't just wishful thinking—it's an ironclad promise found repeatedly in the pages of scripture:

- "Ask and it will be given to you; seek and you will find; knock and the door will be opened to you" (Matthew 7:7 NIV).

- "If you believe, you will receive whatever you ask for in prayer" (Matthew 21:22 NIV).

- "Therefore I say to you, whatever things you ask when you pray, believe that you receive them, and you will have them" (Mark 11:24 NKJV).

- "And whatever you ask in My name, that I will do, that the Father may be glorified in the Son. If you ask anything in My name, I will do it" (John 14:13–14 NKJV).

- "I tell you the truth, you will ask the Father directly, and he will grant your request because you use my name" (John 16:23 NLT).

- "So let us come boldly to the throne of our gracious God. There we will receive his mercy, and we will find grace to help us when we need it most" (Hebrews 4:16 NLT).

- "This is the confidence we have in approaching God: that if we ask anything according to his will, he hears us. And if we know that he hears us—whatever we ask—we know that we have what we asked of him" (1 John 5:14–15 NIV).

The nineteenth-century Anglican bishop J. C. Ryle once said, "Faith is to the soul what life is to the body. Prayer is to faith what breath is to the body. How a person can live and not breathe is past my comprehension, and how a person can believe and not pray is past my comprehension, too."

If you want to see your faith strengthened, you absolutely, positively must spend regular time in prayer. And when you begin to see things happening that wouldn't have happened otherwise, when you learn things you wouldn't have learned without spending time in prayer, your faith will grow—like a snowball rolling down a hill. The more you receive answers to your prayers, the more you'll want to pray. . .and see God do what only He can do.

Endure Tests and Trials of Your Faith—and Thank God for Them

The nineteenth-century evangelist/preacher George Mueller once observed that, "To learn strong faith is to endure great trials. I have learned my faith by standing firm amid severe testings."

Strong words, but scripture repeatedly backs them up.

The Bible contains dozens upon dozens of promises for those who have placed their faith in Jesus Christ. We are promised joy, peace, protection, love, and strength. And let's not forget eternal life! One thing we are *not* promised, however, is that our faith life on this fallen, corrupt world will be easy. On the contrary, the Bible says we will face all kinds of tests, trials, and difficulties—sometimes severe ones.

The apostle James drove home that point when he wrote, "Consider it all joy, my brethren, when you encounter various trials, knowing that the testing of your faith produces endurance. And let endurance have its perfect result, so that you may be perfect and complete, lacking in nothing" (James 1:2–4 NASB).

You may be asking, "How can I find it joyful when life is difficult, when it looks like nothing good can come out of what I'm going through now?"

First of all, understand that the devil won't waste his time on you if you aren't walking in the kind of faith that can change the world around you. On the other hand, Satan will redouble his efforts to thwart a growing faith that threatens to tear down his kingdom here on earth. As a military pilot answered when he was asked how he knew he flying over the right target, "You know because that's when you're being shot at."

If you feel like the world, your circumstances, or the devil himself is unleashing a barrage at you, you can take joy—because it's likely the troubles are coming your way because you're over the right target.

Second, as James points out, the troubles you endure can truly be blessings when you understand that God can and does use them to strengthen your faith, to make you more like Jesus. The apostle Paul drove this promise home when he wrote, "And we know that *all things* work together for good to them that love God, to them who are the called according to his purpose" (Romans 8:28 KJV, emphasis added).

Everyone who lives a life of faith will face difficulties and suffering. That included many, many of the saints whose stories are recorded in the Bible. Here are some examples:

- Joseph—Assaulted by his brothers, sold into Egyptian slavery, and then falsely accused and imprisoned. In the end, he spoke from his heart, "You intended to harm me, but God intended it for good" (Genesis 50:20 NIV).

- Job—The book of Job is the story of a righteous man who, though no fault of his own—and for no reason he could see—suffered the loss of his family, his livelihood, and his physical health.

- King David—Israel's greatest monarch wrote Psalm 31, which lists several instances in which he suffered. Amazingly, David ends this psalm with words of encouragement for all believers: "Oh, love the LORD, all you His saints! For the LORD preserves the faithful, and fully repays the proud person. Be of good courage, and He shall strengthen your heart, all you who hope in the LORD" (Psalm 31:23–24 NKJV).

- Peter and John—Acts 4 reports that the two first-generation apostles were arrested for preaching the name of Jesus and thrown in jail. Yet they told the religious leaders who questioned them the next day that they would not— could not—stop preaching.

- The apostle Paul—You can read about some of Paul's suffering in the book of Acts. Also, in his second letter to the Corinthians, he lists no fewer than forty-five different kinds of suffering he endured.

- Jesus Christ—Jesus lived a sinless, blameless, compassionate life, yet He was falsely accused, betrayed, slandered, beaten, and executed in one of the most horrific manners imaginable—all to pay the price of the sins of humankind.

How can you find joy in your trials? Try looking at them the same way a bodybuilder views the weights he lifts for hours a day, every day. To reach his goals, the bodybuilder has to put himself through pain most of us can't imagine. Does he curse the weights for being heavy? No, because he understands that those weights wear down his muscles so they can come back bigger and stronger than before. If we can look at our trials as weights God allows—even sometimes *causes*—we'll know the ultimate purpose is to make us stronger than we were before.

Someone once said that what doesn't kill you only makes you stronger. That's true in your life of faith. And God has promised that He will *never* test you beyond what He knows you can endure. When you demonstrate just enough faith to allow Him to test you, you can come back from your trials a much stronger man or woman of faith.

Spend Time with Other People of Faith

The Bible clearly teaches the importance of spending time with other believers. There are several good reasons for this, as outlined by the writer of the book of Hebrews: "Let us think of ways to motivate one another to acts of love and good works. And let us not neglect our meeting together, as some people do, but encourage one another, especially now that the day of his return is drawing near" (Hebrews 10:24–25 NLT).

God designed human beings in general—and believers in particular—to need the company of others. The individual Christian receives encouragement and strengthening when he or she spends time with other people of faith. Jesus indicated that when He said, "Truly I tell you that if two of you on earth agree about anything they ask for, it will be done for them by my Father in heaven. For where two or three gather in my name, there am I with them" (Matthew 18:19–20 NIV).

It is amazing what spending time with

other faith-filled believers can do to strengthen and encourage you in your faith. Not only can you communicate with others the struggles and successes you've had, you can observe how God has so faithfully met the needs—spiritual, emotional, financial—of those who have the audacity to believe that He can be counted on to keep each and every one of His promises.

Make it part of your walk of faith to find a good fellowship group, to find a good church to attend, and to spend time with those you know are people of strong and growing faith.

Act On What You Know

Imagine for a moment you are the owner of a small but successful business. You've hired a young man you know has the potential to make your business even more prosperous—but you quickly find out that he doesn't always complete the assignments you give. You know this young employee wants bigger, more important assignments, but you're reluctant to give them to him—because you can't be sure he'll finish them to your satisfaction.

If you don't want to let this talented young man go, you have two choices: Go ahead and promote him, or leave him where he is until he learns how to handle the responsibilities you've already given him. Since you've been running a *successful* business, you know better than to promote the young man—so you leave him where he is until he better applies himself to handling the basics.

The walk of faith is a lot like that. If you think about it, the people you know who have tremendous, mountain-moving faith are probably also people who hear God and obey His commands immediately. You see, part of a life of faith is believing God so firmly and so deeply that you're willing—even eager—to pour yourself into doing what He's asked you to do. And if you don't have enough faith to do the "basics" God has assigned, you can't expect Him to grow your faith enough that He can trust you with bigger tasks.

When you know God wants you to do something—read your Bible more, pray more, repent of some "little" sin—don't wait to act. When you wait, you just delay receiving from God what He wants you to have. But when you step out boldly in obedience, expect Him to send the blessings—including a stronger, life-changing kind of faith.

Be Patient!

More often than not, becoming a mature, faith-filled Christian is a process that requires time and work.

So be patient, keep doing the things the Bible tells you to do, and hold to this amazing promise from the pen of the apostle Paul: "Being confident of this, that he who began a good work in you will carry it on to completion until the day of Christ Jesus" (Philippians 1:6 NIV).

To paraphrase the old bumper sticker, "Be patient with yourself—God is not finished with you yet."

SCRIPTURE INDEX

If you enjoyed
Faith: Back to the Basics,
look for
Explore Your Faith

When you have questions about your faith, turn to *Explore Your Faith*—it provides concise, biblical answers to 75 common questions about the Christian faith. This easy-to-understand guide to faith addresses topics from "How can I know God exists?" and "How can I figure out what God's will is?" to "Why do we have to keep praying for the same thing?" Each entry also includes discussion questions that are great for further study. *Explore Your Faith* will encourage you to dig deeper into your faith—and enhance your spiritual growth!

ISBN 978-1-61626-664-6 / Mass market paperback /
160 pages / $2.99